TESTIFY!

D0992731

THE CONSEQUENCES OF ARCHITECTURE

—

EDITED BY LUKAS FEIREISS
INTRODUCTION BY OLE BOUMAN

NAi PUBLISHERS
NETHERLANDS ARCHITECTURE INSTITUTE

MARIA GRAZIA CUTULI PRIMARY SCHOOL, AFGHANISTAN
Page 134 / 230 / 233

LE 56/ECO-INTERSTICE, FRANCE
Page 98 / 229 / 233

TESTIFY!
THE CONSEQUENCES OF ARCHITECTURE

ESTONOESUNSOLAR, SPAIN
Page 90 / 229 / 233

EICHBAUMOPER, GERMANY
Page 40 / 229 / 233

CINEMA JENIN, PALESTINE
Page 48 / 228 / 233

SKATEISTAN, AFGHANISTAN
Page 116 / 231 / 233

TESTIFY!
THE CONSEQUENCES OF ARCHITECTURE

CONTENTS

INTRODUCTION

ARCHITECTURE AND ITS CONSEQUENCES

Is there anything in today's society that is self-evident, that we do not need to discuss? Nothing seems decisive enough to pre-empt doubts. Reliable certainties are rare and almost nothing can be taken for granted anymore. The language we use, the places we live in, the social classes we belong to, the trades we learn, the institutions we work for, virtually everything and everyone needs to be justified or defended. Confrontational questions are posed every day: Is what you are doing actually relevant or useful? And will it remain so tomorrow? Reality checks like these often result in radical change.

Things are no different for architecture. The complacency with which this profession used to concentrate on producing unique forms and concepts – as well as the attendant publicity – has made way for a renewed interest in the public significance of architecture. At the same time, the unquestionability of the central role the discipline traditionally played in the design and construction of society is fading. As a profession, architecture is now facing serious competition from other specialists in the building process.

As a technique architecture has become part of a chain of construction that reaches beyond its particular expertise. As an art form it is severely criticized as the arcane idiom of an elitist in-crowd. As an economic activity it is being undermined on all sides, and making a decent living in architecture has become a challenge. No wonder the profession is enthusiastically (albeit with a hint of panic) searching for the 'surplus value' of architecture and the 'role of the architect'. It is significant that coming up with precise definitions for these idioms is far from a simple exercise.

—

THE USERS ARE THE WITNESSES YOU NEED TO FIND OUT ABOUT THE QUALITY OF GOOD ARCHITECTURE

—

It may seem sardonic to say that despite these uncertainties, ours is a fantastic age. How privileged we are to live in an era in which we once again have to prove what things are really for and how our actions really matter. How great to stand for an Architecture of Consequence. An architecture the world cannot live without.

The same is true of the Netherlands Architecture Institute, whose principal subject is architecture. The NAI works hard to justify why it organizes a massive programme dedicated to the glory of this discipline every year – through exhibitions that showcase that glory and through the collection of archives maintained on the basis of that glory. This is why the NAI has explicitly made Architecture of Consequence the core of its innovation agenda. If architecture is to be celebrated, collected and discussed, let it be so only as a craft that can prove its indispensability.

In this, the NAI also aims to augment contemporary architecture. This can be done by continually pointing out not just the beauty of architecture, but its genuine accomplishments as well. By asking to what extent architecture provides solutions to our problems it proves itself in the process. It does this by placing architecture in the direct context of the most pressing issues of our time and making the indispensability of architecture irrefutable. Out of all this emerged *Architecture of Consequence* as a long-term programme, a relief operation for architecture, and with it, of course, eventually a relief operation for the NAI itself. After all, a cultural institution that salvages its subject also salvages its own reason for being.

—

ARCHITECTURE IS REINVENTING ITSELF …

—

It has been two years since *Architecture of Consequence* was published as a book. Using projects by Dutch designers, this book demonstrated how much architecture can contribute to the alleviation of great social challenges involving food, health, energy, space and time limitations, social cohesion and value creation. The accompanying exhibition is currently touring around the world, eliciting tremendous response. All over the world, it turns out, there is enormous demand for convincing examples of architecture that provides solutions. In many cases these solutions take the form of social projects, intended to bring about immediate improvement in living conditions, as seen, for instance, in the exhibition 'Small Scale, Big Change' ('in underserved communities'), or the work of Architecture for Humanity. Increasingly, however, projects are responding not to a great need, but to a great opportunity that has long been latent and is suddenly reinterpreted from a new social engagement perspective. This is architecture that proves that all sorts of unexpected possibilities exist for growing food in urban areas, for creating healthy and sustainable environments, supporting social networks and creating real estate value based on new revenue models.

With its innovation agenda, the NAI is frequently asked to present and elucidate this story. It is also regularly asked to calculate the profits achieved, to mediate in finding the right designers for particular projects and to advise on reassessing teaching programmes in this direction. Words, however, are not enough. At its headquarters in Rotterdam, the NAI, uses these reassessments to improve on itself. As of this writing, the last touches are being made to a renovation of the NAI that will make its building more sustainable, more social, more spacious, healthier and more valuable. On top of all of this, a cultural programme is being devised that will end up giving people more time than it costs them. And yet we're not entirely satisfied with our own words and deeds. It's all very well to want to make architecture relevant again in your designs and in discussions, but you can only really 'prove' this if it actually works that way in practice. And to achieve this you have to look beyond intentions and the design analysis. For this you have to listen to the users themselves, those who experience day to day whether your good intentions came true.

—

… NO WONDER WE CAN BE AMAZED AT WHAT IT LOOKS LIKE

—

These users are the witnesses you need in order to judge the quality of good architecture. And because they are users, the point is not a final verdict, but rather an ongoing insight that can be directly put to use in new projects.

These testimonies are the essence of this publication and its accompanying exhibition. The title says it all: *Testify!* Prove that architecture works – not just in its direct function, but also in its programmatic reach, in its cultural effect, and ultimately in its value to society. Demonstrate that architecture solves problems. Show those consequences of architecture. What is most striking is that in judging the success of their everyday surroundings, people do not immediately talk about physical architecture. Their focus is much more on the ways in which their space is organized and therefore how everyday life and its physical backdrop influence each other.

It is therefore no surprise that curator Lukas Feireiss, has ended up choosing designs that some readers may not even recognize as architecture.

That's a risk we're happy to take. Architecture is reinventing itself and it's no wonder that we are amazed at how it looks, at what architecture is, and how it can turn out to be.

REALITY BITES!

EMBRACING THE HUMANE IN ARCHITECTURE

Let's start with a critical diagnosis: there's something wrong with the state of the architecture discourse! It's a three-fold problem. First of all, it's a problem of superficiality: architecture is all too often about a flashy first impression, the primary contact that a building makes with the viewer. Architecture photographers call this the 'money-shot', and these images are usually devoid of any human presence or interaction. The building is the centre of attention, not the people using it or living in it. In the second place, architects suffer from an exclusivity complex, as they deliberately talk only to each other (preferably in highly-conceptual terms). However, discussing architecture solely from the elevated perspective of those who design the buildings ignores a much larger crowd of ordinary users and inhabitants, the people who experience the buildings on a daily basis and who could provide extraordinarily valuable input for the architect – and architects in general – if only they were asked. Finally, a serious educational problem prevails, as architects generally seem to learn alarmingly little from their own buildings.

Most architects never go back to the buildings they designed after they are built, and therefore know very little about their buildings' actual afterlife. Finding out what really happens after a building is finished doesn't seem to be anyone's job.

With these problems in mind, this publication and the accompanying exhibition, *Testify! The Consequences of Architecture,* originally conceived for the Netherlands Architecture Institute in Rotterdam, takes a seemingly humble approach. It aims to literally bring the people back into the picture and then to actually give them a voice, allowing those who live in and use buildings to contribute to a conversation that should have been happening all along. Through this process, the exhibition intentionally challenges the cross-examination of our built environment as the sole provenance of the architect and attempts to interweave architectural discourse into the very fabric of society.

—

FINDING OUT WHAT REALLY HAPPENS AFTER A BUILDING IS FINISHED DOESN'T SEEM TO BE ANYONE'S JOB

—

This book gathers 25 projects from around the globe that have taken the chance to open themselves up to critical self-reflection, submitting to a non-biased evaluation of their work from a lived-in perspective. The selected projects, which are all very recent, range from seemingly straightforward architectural structures to highly experimental and interdisciplinary think-tanks and research groups. Despite their manifold practical and conceptual differences, these projects are all united in an overall attentiveness towards the complex relationships between context and spatial intervention, and a thorough understanding of the transformational power of architecture over time. Pinpointing novel and proactive approaches that draw their conceptual strength from envisioning a combination of multidisciplinary design and its consequences in the built environment, *Testify!* addresses the numerous, current adaptive systems of social, political, ecological and economic challenges and responsibilities that we face today.

All of the featured contributions come together in an inspiring international bandwidth to create a new picture of architectural thinking that considers its own consequences, and that takes our built environment across urban as well as rural landscapes as an example of how to make a problem into a concrete possibility – not only for a solution, but an opportunity to highlight the complex set of factors from which the situation has arisen. It is precisely this consideration of likely consequences that allows those engaged in the spatial design of our society to make choices and decisions that attempt to work towards the best possible outcomes – even if there are no guarantees. Predicting the future can't be done, but we can continue to get more and more accurate by examining what's happened before. Through a closer look at past consequences, a new architecture that considers them pre-emptively, rather than retroactively (if at all), can be created. We look backward only in order to look forward.

—

REALITY MAKES
ANY NEW BUILDING
NECESSARILY UNFINISHED
AND IMPERFECT,
THOUGH PERHAPS
PERFECTIBLE IN TIME

—

In this book, the consequences of architecture are literally narrated by means of first-hand testimonials by and interviews with affected residents, every-day users and involved professionals from extremely diverse backgrounds. Rather than solely presenting architecture from the usual distanced and top-down view of the architect, *Testify!* provides bottom-up entryways into the respective projects and think-tanks via personal stories and individual experiences. Here, school children, workmen and local activists as well as journalists, scientists and politicians have their say – to mention but a few.

In addition to these personal histories of space, a commentary layer of editorial notes unfolds across the overall narrative of the book, providing a critical subtext that gives room for further topical questions and associations. In order to create an easily-approachable and representative image of the contemporary spatial practices featured here, the book is divided into four intergradient thematic chapters.

The first chapter, *Urban Acupuncture. Reprogramming the City*, looks at architectural projects of varying scale that represent built yet often temporary positive interventions within the urban network. In contrast to the first chapter the following chapter, *Smooth Operators. Interventions in the Public Realm*, focuses on amplifying the city's software as opposed to its hardware. The projects in this section offer a collection of informal creative practices within the urban realm and celebrate how these actions continuously contribute to the subversive change of the face of the city today. The third chapter, *Reach Out. Spaces for Learning and Community*, brings together examples of buildings and spaces for learning and schooling, places that simultaneously act as social, cultural and communal catalysts in their respective local contexts. The fourth chapter, *Exploring Horizons. Pushing the Boundaries of Architecture*, looks at various think-tanks and research groups that deliberately stress and question the consequences of architecture beyond disciplinary limitations.

Even though these clusters naturally demarcate the projects, they remain essentially open, inviting exchanges of ideas. They are all distinguished by a flexible, holistic approach throughout the whole planning and design process, as it seems to be clear to them that it has long been impossible for a single profession to deal with creating accomplished architecture in all its complexity, diversity and multifunctionality.

Today, architects see themselves facing new challenges and responsibilities that go well beyond their discipline's horizon of experience. If these challenges are to be met, then an integrative and inclusive approach must be taken to breaking down the boundaries between architecture and other spheres of exterior knowledge and experience. The key to acquiring these new insights is being able to see and think out of the box, and this again offers the opportunity to engage more people from more backgrounds than ever before in the architecture debate and eventually change *how* architecture is discussed.

No evidence suggests that it is a good thing for the critical investigation of architecture to be regarded as an exclusive endeavour reserved only for an esoteric circle of professional insiders, for in fact it should be understood and openly debated across a much broader spectrum. Our entire lives are embedded in architecture. From cradle to grave, we are constantly surrounded, affected and shaped by the structures in which we live – whether consciously perceived or unconsciously experienced. And as much as architecture shapes us, we shape architecture in return – whether professionally trained for it or not. Buildings simply keep changing, because people either have to or want to rework them to suit the unfolding patterns of their lives. As much as an architect would like to understand his or her building as perfect or finished, reality makes any new building necessarily unfinished and imperfect, though perhaps perfectible in time. We can expect the future to be shaped by demographic, social and cultural changes, but what these inevitable changes and their consequences might exactly be, we can only speculate about.

One key to meet the requirements of an ever-changing society in spatial terms, however, is the ability to think and act flexibly over time. This doesn't necessarily mean that a building should be designed so that its purpose can evolve as its needs change over time, but that we essentially remain open towards the unexpected and continue to relish the moment of surprise.

In the same line of thought, American writer Steward Brand, founder of the legendary *Whole Earth Catalogue*, argues in his seminal 1994 book *How Buildings Learn: What Happens After They Are Built* for a time-based learning process by architects, in which 'new usages persistently retire or reshape buildings' and 'function reforms form, perpetually'. The central thesis of his book is essentially what Brand called elsewhere a 'fiasco-by-fiasco-approach to perfection', which describes a profound apprehension of the positive surplus of unsolicited changes, uninvited irritants, and unanticipated setbacks and even failures as the future seeds of human achievement and progress.

So, if anything can be learned from the book currently at hand, apart from deliberately putting people at the centre of the discussion and opening up the all-too elitist architecture debate of today to personal storylines of space, it is that at times detours only broaden one's knowledge of a place. In other words, if we don't get lost every now and then, we haven't moved enough. Sure, not everyone who searches for and misses India discovers America, but mistakes can nevertheless become, as Irish novelist and poet James Joyce tellingly put it, 'the portals to discovery'. At least mistakes clearly show us what needs improvement. And without mistakes, how would we know what we had to work on?

CHAPTER

URBAN ACUPUNCTURE

—

REPROGRAMMING
THE CITY

1

PROJECT
OPEN AIR LIBRARY

ARCHITECT
**KARO* WITH
ARCHITEKTUR+NETZWERK**

LOCATION
**SALBKE-MAGDEBURG,
GERMANY**

TESTIFY!
THE CONSEQUENCES OF ARCHITECTURE

◄ The community-designed structure contrasts with older architecture ▲ View of the library's courtyard area

Page
230 / 233
/ 239

OPEN AIR LIBRARY
SALBKE-MAGDEBURG, GERMANY

A FREE LIBRARY, CONSTRUCTED OVER YEARS OF COMMUNITY INPUT, HAS STABILIZED A DECLINING AREA IN EAST GERMANY, LOOKING TOWARDS THE FUTURE OF THE AREA AND PROVIDING A MODEL FOR FUTURE PROJECTS IN POSTINDUSTRIAL AREAS.

The library is located at a three-way intersection

CONTEXT

Like many other post-communist areas in East Germany, south-east Magdeburg is an urban area characterized by economic decline, abandoned industrial plants, and unused land. The city has high unemployment levels and up to 80 per cent vacancy. In Salbke, Magdeburg's city centre, the buildings are generally intact, but almost totally empty. Shop windows are boarded up and vacant lots have grown over with weeds. The old district library in Salbke was demolished decades ago, leaving an empty lot on the triangular space at the intersection of two main streets.

Despite these positive changes, the library has had to struggle with recurrent acts of vandalism on the weekends by local youth gangs.

MISSION

In 2005, KARO* architects began the project, using an old vacant bakery in Magdeburg's city centre as a base of operations. Working with local residents, the team began asking the community for book donations, and hosted a building workshop in which designs for an open-air library were presented and residents were able to give feedback. Construction of a 'temporary library' began in October 2005, with the aim of garnering support for a permanent structure, uniting community members and attracting attention from local and national authorities. A to-scale model of the selected library design was constructed using 1,000 beer crates, which were lent to the project by a beverage retail company. The temporary library's new shelves were filled with books, and its opening was celebrated with Salbke's first ever poetry slam and readings by well-known authors. The temporary library was only open for two days, but after it was taken down, residents decided to keep the bakery open as a permanent 'reading café'. In a year's time, the bakery's book collection had grown to over 10,000 books. The library's lending system is based on trust – no registration is required, and visitors can take and return books at any time.

The project's aim is to 'stabilize' Salbke's community

REALIZATION

Over time, the success of the initiative attracted the necessary funding from the federal government to construct a permanent open-air library facility in 2009. After a community planning meeting, it became clear to the KARO* team that recycling used materials to build the permanent library was important to Magdeburg residents. For this reason, prefabricated pieces from a recently-demolished warehouse building, originally erected in 1966, were recycled to cover the new building's façade. The structure's main wall has shelving for books and shelters a green space where people can read in the open air, and a raised section houses a cafeteria and a provides a stage where school plays, public readings, concerts and other community events can be held. The reading café still houses the majority of the library's collection – now more than 20,000 books – and the open-air library functions as a community centre where people can gather and read.

In March 2011 the library was vandalized so badly that the structure had to be temporarily closed.

The open-air design and the library's honour system suggest new ideals of institutional transparency and neighbourly cooperation in Magdeburg. The recycled façade symbolically implies a merging of old and new, and allows for a way of addressing, yet transforming, past structures. After the project's professional advisers left Magdeburg, the residents successfully took over the project's management, which is promising for the future of the library. It is too soon to judge the long-term impact of this open-ended experiment. There were some early acts of vandalism that were disappointing to the leaders of the initiative. However, for the first time in years, a few houses in in Salbke have recently been sold, and renovation is underway.

NAME
RAINER MANN

NATIONALITY
GERMAN

OCCUPATION
SALES REPRESENTATIVE

LOCATION
MAGDEBURG, GEMANY

—

As I understand, you are part of the local citizen's group managing the library. Can you tell us more about the overall design and implementation process and how the citizens were involved in it? When the city finally realized that something had to be done about Magdeburg's south-east, architects were sent down here every now and then to come up with solutions. As such, KARO* architects and Sabine Elling-Saalman were asked to plan three empty lots in the centre of Salbke, and we – the citizen's group – acted not only as their local contact on site but also as an integral part of the planning process from the beginning. We, the residents and later users and even the children of the neighbouring elementary school, were completely involved through numerous workshops and were able to contribute to the project with ideas, which were picked up and put to form by the architects. And then, after the planning for the lots had been finished, the most important event for the entire project probably became the installation of the temporary library building, which was made of 2,000 beer crates in one weekend. This temporary and ephemeral structure became the actual moment of birth for the real library building, which now holds 35,000 books. The makeshift structure created an image in the minds of the people that served as a driving force for the at times tedious process to follow. The original design was implemented more or less as planned; cutbacks were only necessary in the technical equipment and the lighting concept, since they were simply not manageable for us financially.

Has the project been well-received by community members and is it self-sustaining at this point?
Despite a few critical opinions about the actual building costs of this very unconventional building, the open-air library has generally been received positively by the community, even though the involvement of the different project partners is rather rare by now, and it's mainly us and the elementary school that are taking care of it. Nevertheless, a number of events have taken place here, such as concerts, open-air church services and choir meetings. It has also been used by the elementary school and during the Christmas season, but due to the fact that the originally planned stereo system was cut from the budget, such events always mean extra costs and effort. Naturally, the building can be used in its function as a library and is used as such, at least in the warmer seasons. Ironically, the city of Magdeburg, which officially declared the library to be part of the IBA (International Building Exhibition), has not organized a single event here. To this very day the city administration actually seems not to really know what to do with the project. By now, however, we are facing a massive vandalism problem by diverse groups of teenagers that regularly occupy the spot as a place to meet and get drunk. This causes problems with the adjacent neighbours. Unfortunately our various attempts to bring those responsible for the vandalism to justice have not been greatly supported by the police. But apart from all that, it's also important to recognize the fact that during the building process of the library, the surrounding area was redesigned as well, which raised the overall appearance of the location and even led to the sale of two vacant buildings. Two adjacent home-owners even renovated their façades and another building is now about to do the same. But generally speaking, it seems that the open-air library is noticed and recognized much more abroad then it is here in Magdeburg.

NAME
STEPHAN WILLINGER

NATIONALITY
GERMAN

OCCUPATION
FEDERAL INSTITUTE FOR RESEARCH ON BUILDING, URBAN AFFAIRS AND SPATIAL DEVELOPMENT, BONN

LOCATION
BONN, GERMANY

—

Working for the department of urban development in germany you have supported the project from its beginning. Could you

elaborate on your first impression of the city? Magdeburg-Salbke and its surrounding area is a perfect example of a so-called shrinking city, typical of the dramatic development in eastern Germany since 1989, which has led to an extreme population decline and more than a million empty apartments and the abandonment of countless industrial parks and social and cultural facilities. I was rather shocked when I first came to the city in the summer of 2006. I could hardly imagine how an urban design process of this moderate a scale could bring a positive change to this kind of area. But after talking to the people who actually live there and feeling there engaging and dynamic appropriation of urban places and their strong will to make a change, I was really impressed. Despite the fact that their youth is almost completely moving further west, and that this village on the periphery of Magdeburg is not very attractive in itself, they were enthusiastic from the beginning. This strong engagement is what eventually convinced us to donate money to support the library. We hoped it could really become a prototype for similar projects in other parts of Germany.

The attitude of the residents seems of paramount importance. The first step was really the cooperation of the community – people have to believe that change is possible, and trust the architects, before anything can begin. Yes, this was very much the case in Salbke. As part of the federal restructuring programme, KARO* organized an initial event directed towards the public that really became the key moment for the entire process, because at the end of it the participating people could already see the results of their engagement. It made them aware of what could be possible for the future. It was through this weekend event, which included poetry readings and performances of all sorts, that a collec-

tive vision was created and nurtured during the whole process of three to four years before the building was actually finished.

It was a long project from start to finish. How did the administration help in the process? There was a lot of scepticism from the local administration in Magdeburg, because they had never done a project like this before. It was very interesting for me to see and understand that city administrations really need to learn from scratch how to realize projects with such a high level of community engagement and involvement. This is very different to the way they are used to working. Usually, a master planner comes in, makes an urban design, has it built, congratulates himself when the project is finished, and says how happy everyone is. End of story. Here, a community process was in full effect, in which the architect has a completely new role as a mediator and translator. The architect does not present a finished design but actually asks the people in numerous workshops to participate and help him with the design. There were quite a few unnecessary complications and problems, simply because the administration wasn't used to this kind of collaborative process. Sure, this type of collaboration is a rare case, but cities with little money in particular should open themselves up to it! In a village like Salbke, they don't have the funds to come up with a big design solution, so they have to regard architecture and urban planning more and more as social processes that utilize the social network of the neighbourhood. It's a new thing, but they will have to get used to it sooner or later.

You describe the architects as mediator and translators. Could you elaborate on that notion? The architects' role in this project was very special, in the sense that they as the architects managed to seamlessly

combine the participatory process with the design process though involving the citizens literally from beginning to end. The architects were not at all telling the people what to do, but rather trying to help them figure it out themselves. Let me give you an example: the residents wanted to use recycled materials for the design. KARO* picked up on the idea of recycling and alternatively suggested the reuse of another material, namely the old storefront façade elements that have eventually been used for the library. So they really listened and provided constructive feedback, and were at no point just saying yes or no. It's a very brave stance to take as an architect, but I think one can really learn from it. To me Salbke is in that sense a role model for combining a participatory process with an ambitious architectural design. Against the backdrop of the numerous small communities with little money throughout Germany and also abroad that face similar problems to those in Salbke, there is a real need to engage citizens more and more in the design and management of public spaces. It is my hope that this can be done anywhere.

So what's your verdict? I guess you can't expect to change the whole economic and social condition of a neighbourhood with one intervention in public space. But you can try to stabilize and foster the existing social networks, and bring the young and the old together to sit and discuss their shared environment. Really, the greatest success of this project is that the citizens made it and still manage it.

PROJECT
PROJECT ROW HOUSES

CREATOR
RICK LOWE

LOCATION
HOUSTON, TEXAS, USA

Barack Hussein Obama, 2006

PROJECT ROW HOUSES
HOUSTON, TEXAS, USA

BEGINNING WITH THE RENOVATION OF A ROW OF SHOTGUN-STYLE HOUSES IN HOUSTON'S THIRD WARD, RICK LOWE, ALONG WITH THE NEIGHBOURHOOD COMMUNITY AND HUNDREDS OF VISITING CREATIVE PEOPLE, HAS TRANSFORMED THE STREET INTO A VIBRANT CULTURAL HUB, AND IN TURN DEVELOPED A LONG LIST OF SOCIAL PROGRAMMES TO PROVIDE ASSISTANCE TO THE UNDERPRIVILEGED THROUGH ART AND EDUCATION.

CONTEXT

Project Row Houses (PRH) began in 1993 as a result of discussions among African-American artists in Houston who wanted to establish a positive, creative presence in their own community. Artist and community activist Rick Lowe spearheaded the pursuit of this vision when he discovered the abandoned site of 22 'shotgun'-style houses in Houston's Third Ward. The project explores creative ways to preserve and redevelop a historic site in a low-income neighbourhood just over 1.5 km from the centre of downtown Houston.

MISSION

The concept for the project takes inspiration from the work of two distinct artists: Joseph Beuys and John Biggers. Joseph Beuys's theory of social sculpture influenced Lowe's decision to explore the community as an art project. John Biggers, a Houston artist, made many paintings depicting African-American life in Houston, including shotgun house communities. These small houses with gabled roofs have a particular interior layout in which all doorways are aligned. They were known in America's south as shotgun houses, purportedly because a shotgun could be fired straight through the house without touching anything inside. Through research and interviews with Biggers, Lowe became fascinated by the contradicting perspectives surrounding the shotgun house – while many declared that the Third Ward's row of shotgun houses symbolized the stagnation of the community, Biggers' paintings celebrated the houses' architectural form and

Beuys created the term Social Sculpture to illustrate his idea of art's potential to transform society. As a work of art it includes human activity, which strives to structure and shape society or the environment. To him art and activities related to art are the 'only evolutionary-revolutionary power'.

their potential to house vibrant communities. The basis of the PRH concept was to develop a community by reviving the abandoned houses, keeping emphasis on creativity, education and economic sustainability.

REALIZATION

Major challenges at the beginning were the lack of financial resources, a general public disdain for the shotgun houses, and city officials who were determined to demolish 'the worst place in the community' rather than attempt to transform it. The strategy began with the houses themselves – it was necessary to call attention to the architecture in a way that challenged negative stereotypes and demonstrated their historical relevance. Without financial resources, human resources were vital; artists volunteered to help clean up the site, and soon afterwards community youth joined in, followed eventually by their parents and other community members. After six months of weekend work, the beauty of the architecture began to emerge.

The project needed broad support if it was to be sustainable. To introduce the project to the broader community and represent the architecture in a positive light, artists were invited to reflect on the history of the community by creating paintings on the boards that covered the windows and doors. This was called the 'Drive By' exhibition. With the knowledge that most people from outside the community would be afraid to get out of their cars in such a neighbourhood, the idea was to make work that could be seen from a car window.

▲ A piece by artist Sam Durant for one of the converted row houses

▼ Reaching out to the local community through art initiatives

Further exhibitions were developed as an ongoing way of creatively engaging the community, which in turn generated greater appreciation for the relevance of the shotgun house as an architectural form as well as awareness of its particular cultural history.

During the past 17 years, over 400 artists, architects and other creative people have engaged the project and community through the Artist Projects Program, using 12 of the 22 houses for artist projects and studios. The project responded to the need for youth involvement by organizing a summer and after-school programme to engage community youth and use an arts-based curriculum to nurture creativity. Additionally, a transitional housing programme was established to connect the project with other needs expressed by community residents; in seven of the 22 houses, the Young Mothers Residency Program provides assistance to young, single mothers who are completing degrees and supporting their families. The innovation of Project Row Houses is that a wide range of professionals was lead by artists to implement a ground-up development within a neighbourhood that no one was willing to invest in. While the impetus for the project came from outside of the community, the local community was quickly brought into the process through engagement with artists, education programmes and housing initiatives. The project continues to focus on direct engagement of community residents as the source of guiding the ongoing growth of the project.

After getting Project Row Houses off the ground, Lowe came to LA in 1994 and tried to do the same in Watts. As a result, the grassroots non-profit Watts House Project enlisted neighbourhood residents and volunteer artists to turn a row of 20 homes facing the Watts Towers into an aesthetically engaging place to visit and live.

—

THE WORK WAS MADE SO THAT IT COULD BE SEEN FROM A CAR, SINCE MOST PEOPLE FROM OUTSIDE THE COMMUNITY WOULD BE AFRAID TO GET OUT OF THEIR CARS IN SUCH A NEIGHBOURHOOD

—

▼ An installation by artist Sherman Fleming

▶ Crowd at the opening of a Project Row Houses event

TESTIFY!
THE CONSEQUENCES OF ARCHITECTURE

NAME
ASSATA-NICOLE RICHARDS

NATIONALITY
AMERICAN

OCCUPATION
**PROGRAMME COORDINATOR AND
RESEARCHER, PROJECT ROW HOUSES**

LOCATION
HOUSTON, TEXAS, USA

Please describe how you learned about the project and became involved in it. I was living in Houston's Third Ward when the Young Mothers Residential Program (YMRP) of Project Row Houses (PRH) was starting in 1996. A former neighbour initially told me about the programme and encouraged me to apply. At the time, my housing situation was very tenuous. I was living in a two-bedroom duplex with my son and six other individuals in the poorest section of the neighbourhood.

What were your expectations for the project before it began? Considering my housing situation, my first expectation was to have a comfortable, safe and appealing place to live with my son. It would be the first time in a very long time that we would have the stability that would allow me to create a nurturing environment for both of us. My second expectation was to be provided an opportunity to return to school as a full-time student after having dropped out on academic probation four years earlier. Since leaving the University of Houston after my third semester, I'd been forced to work 40 hours a week or more to provide for myself and my son. Not only was my self-esteem low, but my resources were extremely limited and I did not have the means to change our circumstances on my own.

Exactly what was your experience with the project? I started the YMRP in the winter of 1996 and completed the programme in the late summer of 1997. The programme was intensive in a number of ways. I was immersed in a community within the Project Row Houses organization with four other women and their children. I met on a weekly basis with the programme director to outline my personal short-term and long-term goals, as well as address any obstacles that arose to prevent me from obtaining these goals.

These individual meetings required me to address unresolved issues that were unidentified as roadblocks in my life. Furthermore, I met with the other mothers weekly for workshops on various topics to further assist our development. I also attended regularly scheduled events, such as exhibition openings, plays, dinners, concerts and other social outings. An additional requirement was for me to participate in PRH's Public Art Program. This involved volunteering, attending the project openings, artists' talks and other events. It was through this that art became an integral part of my and my son's lives. It became the seed of our transformations. Simply put, our lives changed from being a constant battle with pressures from our environment to a place of stability, nurturing and creativity.

Do you have regular contact with the other participants? Yes, I'm very connected to the other participants. Specifically, I'm very close to the mothers that I participated in the programme with in 1996. We forged relationships with each other that have endured. We get together with our children on a regular basis to celebrate our accomplishments and provide continual support for each other. Because we see our time at Project Row Houses as pivotal and at the centre of what holds us together, we continue to talk about the process and its lasting effects on us, as well as about how the programme is impacting current participants.

How did things change from beginning to end? As I stated, I entered the YMRP with the key goal of returning to school. Because I had left college on academic probation, my confidence in my academic abilities was extremely low. The difficulties that I had faced providing for myself and my son had increased my doubts that I could ever complete my education.

'I FEEL A SENSE OF OBLIGATION TO OFFER THE BEST THAT I HAVE, TO GIVE BACK TO THE ORGANIZATION AND COMMUNITY THAT HAS GIVEN ME SO VERY MUCH'

However, the supportive environment of the YMRP helped to restore my belief that I could be successful academically. I was given constant encouragement and resources to return to the University of Houston as a determined and committed full-time student. When I encountered challenges, I began to feel confident that I had the internal and external tools to manage them. With a stable environment, I was able to dedicate the necessary time and energy to be an accomplished student, as well as a present parent. As a consequence of the YMRP, I graduated with honours for my bachelor's degree, and went on to earn my doctorate in Sociology. After finishing my education, I taught at the University of Pittsburgh as an assistant professor. Recently, I decided to return to Houston and Project Row Houses to live and work. I feel a sense of obligation to offer the best that I have, to give back to the organization and community that has given me so very much.

Finally, the intensive programming of the YMRP transformed me as a person and as a parent. I learned the necessary skills to nurture myself and my son mentally, physically and emotionally. Empowered to make better decisions about our daily lives and futures, I was determined to maintain the standard of living that we were offered at Project Row Houses. This standard involved the physical structure of a home, but, just as importantly, it meant the social safety net of the community of other single-parent mothers. We learned to support each other to reduce the burden of raising our children in single-parent households. We became each other's best resources and allies. As a result of what Project Row Houses gave me, my son developed into an actor and dancer with a number of other talents. Most of all, he has entered adulthood as a whole person, with the necessary foundation to have a successful life that he can define for himself.

What is the future of the project? What are your hopes for it? Have you stayed involved? Does it aim to be self-sustaining?

Currently, I am the YMRP coordinator, which feels very surreal. I sometimes have a feeling of disbelief that I have been able to overcome the many obstacles standing in the way of achieving the goals that I had set for myself.

I have so many hopes for the YMRP, which is already in its fifteenth year. My central hope is that the programme continues to provide the support and resources necessary to give young mothers the opportunity to transform their lives and the lives of their children for many more years to come. Looking towards the future, I hope that we will be able to develop a non-residential component to the programme that offers on-going support to these families when they transition out of the programme. This long-term support is critical because we recognize that the two years that most of our mothers spend in the residential programme is only a beginning. Therefore, we want to sustain this foundation by assisting them with developing and sustaining support systems that endure across time and place. Furthermore, a non-residential component will allow us to serve a larger number of single mothers and their children. I also hope that alumni of the YMRP continue to feel a sense of responsibility to ensure the longevity of the programme. Our personal successes are testaments to the fact that investing in women and children results in substantial individual and societal benefits. Finally, I hope that the YMRP is given greater recognition as a national model for how the arts can both serve and build community.

PROJECT
EICHBAUMOPER

ARCHITECT
RAUMLABOR BERLIN

LOCATION
**MÜHLHEIM/RUHR,
GERMANY**

▲ Eichbaum's subway platform became a stage

▼ A bird's-eye view of Eichbaum station

EICHBAUMOPER MÜHLHEIM/RUHR, GERMANY

THE RAUMLABORBERLIN TEAM REALIZED THE SEEMINGLY IMPOSSIBLE GOAL OF CONVERTING A METRO STATION INTO AN OPERA HOUSE. THROUGH EDUCATIONAL PROGRAMMES AND CULTURAL INTERVENTIONS, THE PREVIOUSLY UNSAVOURY AREA HAS BECOME A THRIVING POINT OF DIALOG AND EXCHANGE.

CONTEXT

The construction of the U18 underground subway line between the cities of Mülheim and Essen signified the modernization and mobilization of Western Germany's Ruhrgebiet area 30 years ago. The Eichbaum (Oak tree) subway station at the centre of the U18 line was seen as a prime example of modern architecture. Today, the Eichbaum station is notorious only for violence and vandalism. The tunnels and entrances leading to the platforms are dark and unsafe, even during the day. The local public transport authority has been trying to deal with the place for years, and attempts have been made to upgrade security by establishing fences at the entrances, installing video cameras, and painting the walls to create a friendlier atmosphere. However, the station has so far resisted all attempts to improve it.

MISSION

The 'Eichbaumoper' (Oak tree opera) transformed the Eichbaum station into an opera house. In an on-site experiment, an innovative opera was created in collaboration with various specialists, inspired by direct interaction with the people who use the station. During the research phase of the project, team members spoke to area residents, gathering stories and ideas. Additionally, they conducted interviews with public transport officials and those involved with the initial construction of the subway. Urban planning aspirations appeared in stark contrast to the everyday experiences of normal people. It was with this in mind that the Berlin-based Raumlabor team attempted to reappropriate the subway's central station via a fantastic operatic production. The production process was focused on the inter-connection of architecture, theatre, music and urban environment, with the ultimate goal of trans-forming space through modifying daily interaction with it. Changing the public perception and uniting people around the project was key to making a nicer, safer public space.

In order to carry on the momentum of the successful implementation of the Eichbaumoper, Raumlabor Berlin has now submitted a proposal for a strategic master plan entitled Eichbaumpark, aimed at creating a long-term solution for the area, to the German Federal Ministry for Transport, Building and Urban Development.

REALIZATION

While action, rather than structural intervention, was the focus of the plan, a small building was constructed near the entrance of the station. The 'Opernbauhütte' served as a base for operations, as well as a working space for artists and residents. Composed of old shipping containers, the building's unusual shape and dramatic presence changed the atmosphere of the Eichbaum area, and over time the building's uses expanded and changed. It became a stage from which to present interim results of work, a project centre for community workshops, and a laboratory for discussion. The Opern-bauhütte will remain at Eichbaum for the long term.

Three composers and three authors worked on location. The authors collaborated to write a three-part opera about local people and specific matters affecting the city, to which the composers added music. An open call for singers was held, and training workshops with professionals were offered. In June 2009, the first opera debuted, using the entire Eichbaum station as its stage. A temporary grandstand that could accommodate 200 audience members was built over the platform, and the whole station was kept open to the public during the event to maximize viewership.

From its inception, the Eichbaumoper was meant to be a truly versatile venue. It has since been converted into an arena for a boxing championship and a rap battle, and soccer matches are projected at the station for fans to come and watch together. The space has been transformed further by artists, who were invited to come and paint dingy surfaces, and art workshops have allowed the community's youth to get involved in adding visual appeal to the formerly barren structure. A monthly periodical, Die Eichbaumoper, has documented and publicized activities and progress and provided a forum for local participants to voice their ideas and communicate with each other. The realization and success of the Eichbaumoper has led to tangible changes in the community. The neglected and unpleasant subway station has turned into a place of possibilities and a centre for cultural activity and community action.

—

THE ABANDONED AND UNPLEASANT SUBWAY STATION HAS TURNED TO A PLACE OF POSSIBILITIES AND A CENTER FOR CULTURAL ACTIVITY AND COMMUNITY ACTION

—

▲ The 'Opernbauhütte' built from cargo-containers will permanently remain on-site

▼ The station has been a venue for many events, from boxing to rap battles

–
NAME
ROBIEN SCHMIDT

NATIONALITY
GERMAN

OCCUPATION
STUDENT

LOCATION
MÜHLHEIM, GERMANY
–

What's the area of the Eichbaum like? The Eichbaum is a rather unfriendly metro station between the cities of Essen and Mühlheim that is mainly frequented by school kids on their way to or back from school. In the 1980s there were a lot of violent attacks in and around the station, which have influenced the common perception of the place to this day and surely did not help the overall reputation of this space in the community. The area around Eichbaum is also characterized by extreme social differences. There are social housing blocks to the north with residents of mainly emigrational background on the one hand, and literally on the other there are small single-family houses inhabited by more well-off people. However, as both are living so close to one another, the Eichbaum becomes the common ground where both groups meet when using the infrastructure of the public transport system. This actually quite often leads to clashes. That's why the Eichbaum area has never really been accepted or even used by the community at all apart from its function as regional metro station. If anything, it served as a kind of hangout for kids to spray paint, hang out and drink beer. And that in its turn caused a lot of elder people to prefer taking the car or bus and avoid using the metro station.

How did you get involved?
I first came in touch with the project through my grandmother, with whom I live in the first house next to the station. She wanted to participate as an extra in the Eichbaumoper. Since opera's never really been my cup of tea, I didn't show much interest. But then passing by everyday on my way to school, I saw the project gradually develop. More and more people showed up. And when they started a project for the local youth here, I eventually started to get involved. At one point I even came up with the idea to form a real club in order to make sure that this place and its programme remains for us teenagers in the long term. In the course of the first year, I ended up spending every day here, did an official internship at raumlaborberlin and took care of everything that needed to be taken care of.

How has the space been used ever since? The container really served as some kind of cell or seed of possibilities, out of which all other projects grew. But it also serves as a social gathering space, in particular, but not only, for the local youth to meet and spend time together, as it provides protection from the rain and cold. All kinds of events and parties went down here. I, for example, celebrated my twentieth birthday here with friends, and recently we had an exhibition of a local high school inside the container. The small film screening programme we offer here is also very well received and last year a lady from the neighbourhood self-initiated a public party for children at the Eichbaum. It is a great feeling to know that we will be able to keep this place alive for the people. We're still in regular contact with the architects, but it's now really up to us to keep it going. I even joined a national youth council that aims to support and provide role model projects like the Eichbaumoper. We meet with politicians of the Federal Ministry to discuss how to best support such projects in the long term and how to give a voice to the needs and wishes of the youth today.

—
'THE CONTAINER REALLY SERVED AS SOME KIND OF CELL OR SEED OF POSSIBILITIES, OUT OF WHICH ALL OTHER PROJECTS GREW'
—

–
NAME
ULRIKE SEYBOLD

NATIONALITY
GERMAN

OCCUPATION
PRODUCTION AND MANAGEMENT ASSISTANT

LOCATION
BOCHUM, GERMANY
–

How did the project originate and how was the first contact with the community established by the architects? The Eichbaumoper project originated in 2006 when the architects Jan Liesegang and Matthias Rick of raumlaborberlin discovered the Eichbaum and its history as part of a larger mission to explicitly find a space of hope in the Ruhrpott region.
The architects came up with the idea to trigger a transformational process in this derelict non-space, which seems to have given up all hope for change.
I joined the project in autumn of 2008, when the work and ideas began to be communicated to the surrounding residents and the overall community. At that point we started to talk to the people and gather their stories for the opera. One of the nice things about the whole opera project is that it was written based on the stories the residents and participants provided about this place. It reflected their everyday experiences, and was actually integrated into them as well, as all the rehearsals

and even the premiere itself were held during the normal running hours of the metro line. In the beginning it was my job to learn everything about the place and communicate it as well as possible to the composers and writers of the opera. At the same time, I was involved in getting more and more local residents interested in what we were doing and eventually interested in even participating in the project. This was partly achieved via classical means such as flyers, posters and press statements, but mainly through our continuous presence on site. The container was set up in November of 2008 but the premiere of the opera was not until the summer of 2009. So, the concept was as simple as saying: here we are, the doors are open, we have coffee and cookies and you are invited to step in, we're interested in talking to you and in hearing your ideas for this place.

—
'THE MAIN DESIGN WAS NOT ENGAGED ON A SPATIAL OR ARCHITECTURAL BUT ON A SOCIAL LEVEL'
—

Can you describe the design process a bit from your perspective? The original design was conceived and built by raumlaborberlin. But the resulting container architecture was intended as a neutral frame for a canvas to be created

through participatory interactions with the local residents. The architecture's aim was to leave as much freedom as possible for changes and adaptations by the local community. Together with a group of teenagers we built all kinds of things here and even invited them to spray paint the exterior of the container. The main design, however, was not engaged on a spatial or architectural but on a social level. Along with both of the main projects here, a wide-ranging programme of events and activities was offered. A series of smaller happenings and workshops always preceded and followed the main events. We even edited and printed a number of issues of a special Eichbaum newspaper that we put together with the residents and participants.

Beyond its physical presence, has the project had an effect on the community? I very much believe so. Two and a half years of work on site have had an impact on the community in a larger sense. From the very start it was the architects' explicit goal to eventually hand over the project to the local community. For me it was interesting to see how deeply fears and stereotypes about this place were rooted in the heads of many residents, but how it has nevertheless proven possible to dissolve these prejudices over time. It just takes a lot of patience and continuity as well as stubbornness. Even those residents that did not participate in any of the projects or were even sceptical about them, now recognize that places can really change. We often hear comments from these people like: 'Well, I do not really know what you are doing here, but I know that it feels much safer since you are here.' Apart from that, the project really brought people together and established friendships across diverse social backgrounds. It's great to see that sometimes the impossible is possible.

PROJECT
CINEMA JENIN

CREATOR
CINEMA JENIN E.V.

LOCATION
JENIN, PALESTINE

CINEMA JENIN
JENIN, PALESTINE

A RENOVATED AND RECONSTRUCTED CINEMA, SUPPORTED BY A NON-PROFIT ORGANIZATION CONSISTING OF FILM MAKERS, CULTURAL ADVOCATES AND INVESTORS, INSPIRES HOPE AND PROVIDES A SPACE FOR EDUCATION AND CULTURAL PRODUCTION IN AN ISOLATED AND WAR-TORN AREA OF PALESTINE.

CONTEXT

The Jenin governorate, about 80 km north of Jerusalem, is home to roughly 230,000 inhabitants. The city of Jenin and its adjacent refugee camp were the site of fierce fighting during Palestine's Second Intifada, and consequentially the region suffers from isolation on economic, social and cultural levels. Though Jenin was once a centre of commerce, its unemployment rate has risen to nearly 80 per cent in recent years. Options for leisure time and cultural activities are severely limited. Most citizens under the age of 20 have never seen a movie on a cinema screen. The only media outlet is television and, for those who have access to a computer, the Internet. Jenin's old cinema was a large building constructed in the early 1960s and surrounded by a vast garden. It had about 155 seats on the first floor and another 180 on a balcony with private booths. However, since its closure more than 20 years ago, the cinema had been used as a dump and was in a deplorable condition. The wooden chairs were in a state of advanced decay, the old 35mm projectors were unusable, and the projection screen had been torn up. The building and all of the equipment were in need of repair or replacement.

The nearest cinema is in the city of Nablus, 40 km away. Movement restrictions due to the occupation render it practically out of reach for many of Jenin's inhabitants.

MISSION

The story began in 2005, when Ahmed Khatib, an 11-year-old resident of the Jenin refugee camp, was killed by the Israeli army. Ahmed's father, Ismael Khatib, decided to donate his son's organs to save the lives of wounded children, several of whom were Israeli. A year later, still deeply affected by his son's death, Khatib opened a cultural centre for the children of the camp.

With the aid of foreign donations, the camp was able to begin providing many activities for youth, including film courses. Khatib's story captured the world's media attention and is told in German director Marcus Vetter's award-winning documentary The Heart of Jenin.

But while the movie was celebrated internationally, Jenin was lacking a place where its very own story could be told. The children from Khatib's cultural centre wanted to produce their first short film, but realized that they would have no place to show it in. The old cinema in the centre of the city was originally built in the early 1960s, and was formerly one of the largest and best-known cinemas of the region, until it was closed at the beginning of the first Intifada in 1987. Cinema Jenin e.V. was founded in 2008 by a collaborative group of German and Palestinian enthusiasts to tackle the project of bringing a derelict cinema back to life and to return a piece of everyday life to the people of Jenin. Given that Jenin's population is extremely young (42.3 per cent of the refugee camp's population is under the age of 15), programmes that cultivate creativity and promote productive activity for young people have the potential to make a huge difference to the area's future.

The overall goal of Cinema Jenin is to break apart the situation of isolation and lack of perspective in Jenin through creating sustainable change and improved living conditions. This aim encompasses a multitude of objectives in three core areas. First of all, the cinema will promote cultural and social integration by re-esta-blishing a cinema-going culture in the city, integrating the city of Jenin and the adjacent refugee camp, providing a venue for local artistic talent, and raising awareness for the rights of women and children.

▲ Jenin has few public gathering places

▼ The cinema's courtyard has been renovated for outdoor meetings and screenings

The cinema provides a stage for performances of all kinds

Second, the cinema will foster an environment of peace and a real intercultural dialogue, by opening a window to the outside world in times of occupation and siege, providing a place for cultural self-expression and exchange of ideas, reintegrating Jenin into regional and international cultural exchange, and encouraging principles of coexistence and conversation-based conflict resolution. Lastly, the cinema has the tangible goal of creating educational opportunities and strengthening the economy. The project will provide technical education and educational screenings for school classes, create sustainable jobs for Jenin citizens, increase the attractiveness of Jenin as a possible tourist and business destination, and sow the seeds for a local film industry.

REALIZATION
It was decided at an early stage to spend the donations received for the project as locally as possible. There are many reasons why this is fairly uncommon for building projects in Palestine; working nearly exclusively with local craftsmen is far more complicated and more trying than authorizing one large company.

—

THE OVERALL GOAL OF CINEMA JENIN IS TO BREAK APART THE SITUATION OF ISOLATION AND LACK OF PERSPECTIVE IN JENIN

—

Openings at the cinema are often highly-publicized events

The Cinema Jenin team worked with numerous small businesses and one-person enterprises that had to be coordinated, and it was often challenging to find someone for each step who was capable of doing the job proficiently, reliably and accurately. Although there is a large pool of labour in Jenin due to high unemployment rates, fragmentary education and years with no job prospects have allowed for little on-the-job experience. The team had not anticipated all of the potential miscommunications that would arise because of cultural differences and political conflict in the area.

The Western team, used to settling matters quickly via phone or email, had to get used to the cultural habit of extensively discussing issues in personal meetings.

Over time, the newcomers learned from the Palestinians' ability to deal with adverse conditions, imponderables and endless inconvenience. The team's Palestinian counterparts always managed to find a way to reroute carefully planned procedures that had seemed inflexible. It was through this way of working together and adopting one another's abilities that the team became a part of Jenin and the cinema truly became a local project.

The cinema's opening inauguration film was Heart of Jenin, the movie that started it all. The programme went on with fascinating Arab and international films and exceptional concerts, with a wide-ranging children's programme rounding up the festival.

From the very beginning of Cinema Jenin, it was clear that only an organization that could sustain itself would be able to bring about lasting change in Jenin. A serious part of the planning process was aimed at achieving long-term sustainability in the economic, employment and social areas. The local team involved in the renovation process is now acting as the core management team, and between ten and 20 international volunteers are so far remaining in Jenin to secure the transference of technical and organizational knowledge. Cinema Jenin has become a symbol of successful cooperation for a nonviolent and independent future. The large numbers of people who have travelled to Jenin for the project were surprised at their positive experiences, and positive media attention is a sign of growing sympathy for the local population. Jenin citizens are finding a way to create their own future.

NAME
DAGMAR QUENTIN

NATIONALITY
GERMAN

OCCUPATION
**PROJECT MANAGER,
CINEMA JENIN**

LOCATION
JENIN, PALESTINE

–

Can you describe the situation when you first came to Jenin?
We came here for the first time almost three years ago with the somewhat naive idea to do peace work, but it's so much more complex than any of us ever expected. Jenin is a city in the occupied territory, where the people suffered a lot and the occupied and the occupiers by no means see eye-to-eye. Against this backdrop, we are naturally facing countless problems, as we are also trying to deliberately bring Palestinians and Israelis closer through our project. Rumours even say that we are working for the Israelis as part of their so-called normalization programme. A lot of people are suspicious because we have fundraised around one million euros for the project and it is hard for anyone here to believe that we are not putting this money in our own pockets.

Despite all the difficulties you obviously managed to create quite a momentum for this project. How did you achieve this? Yes, in the beginning everybody was extremely supporting and generous. The idea of reopening this derelict cinema after more than 20 years in Palestine struck a chord with so many people from all over the world. Rodger Waters of Pink Floyd, for example, gave us 160,000 euros of his private money. That's incredible. Now, we do have an intact cinema, but we're still facing so many problems and we still need money in order to keep it running. It's sobering to see that often it's much easier to stir up the initial energy for an ambitious project such as ours, but it's much, much more challenging to truly sustain it over the long run. One wouldn't think so, but it's so much more difficult to raise funds for the cinema now that it exists than it was before the opening. The ordinary, the everyday proves to be the real challenge. As we don't really generate income, we can't properly promote the cinema. We should print flyers and posters, we should be on TV

or at least on the local radio stations. It's a bit of a vicious circle at times.

As a both a foreigner and woman in Palestine, how did you establish yourself there? Our approach was to include the context from the beginning, by offering workshops to the locals. To simply get them acquainted with how to show a movie, for instance. Over time we've had a lot of enthusiastic people from the neighbourhood working with us. As a result we've been well accepted by the community. The local community has been very appreciative and generous. I, for example, have been literally adopted by a local family, and I am invited more or less every night to sleep over. Being adopted is the biggest sign of trust you can get around here. You become part of their family and you live and eat with them. However, what proves to be really difficult at times is not so much our acceptance, but the acceptance of the people who work at the cinema. We once had a manager who was not from town, which turned out to be a huge problem. He was not well received at all. People were jealous because most of them have nothing; 60 per cent are unemployed and if they see someone else with a piece of the cake, they want their share. Therefore we are now in the phase of changing people and getting many more locals involved, which simply wasn't possible at the beginning because we just didn't have the same relationships with the people here that we do now.

What role does the medium film play in Jenin? Do you think the cinema will be used for other events as well? People here actually do not read very much, nor do they watch films at all. Sure, this is partly due to the fact that there has been no cinema around for more than 20 years, but apart from that, the people are simply not used to concentrating

'YOU HAVE TO UNDERSTAND, THESE PEOPLE ARE UNDER CONSTANT AND PERMANENT STRESS. THEY'RE NOT USED TO SITTING DOWN ON A CHAIR AND FOLLOWING A STORY FOR ONE AND A HALF HOURS'

—

on a feature film from beginning to end. In particular if it is a challenging storyline. You have to understand, these people are under constant and permanent stress. They're not used to sitting down on a chair and following a story for one and a half hours. They'd rather watch television series at home. We didn't realize this before we came. I think for Markus Vetter, the director of the documentary The Heart of Jenin and initiator of the entire project here, it was probably surprising to understand that the normal people here do

not care so much about high-quality documentaries from around the globe. You naturally can't start with an art house film programme here, but rather with Arabic films, which are often very simple love and drama stories. We also have the Muslim factor to consider, meaning that we can't show films with kissing or even with girls wearing shirts with spaghetti straps, for example. But leaving the whole film discussion aside, what people here generally love is music and dancing and we can offer a big stage for that

as well. The cinema is not only for showing movies but offers a place for social and communal gathering. In the summer we even have the enclosed garden in the back, which is wonderful. A public space like that is rare, or rather nonexistent here. In addition we are currently working on a new educational curriculum including an empowerment programme for women, as well as collaboration with an organic baker from Germany who will take in apprentices from around here, and a course for construction workers about new technologies and materials.

What have you learned over the course of the last years and what is your perspective for the project?
I would be lying if I'd tell you that the cinema is exactly what we hoped for. A project like this must be understood as a work in progress. We have learned enormously just by trying things out and making a lot of mistakes. Right now we are in a transitional phase, as we eventually want to hand it all over to the Palestinians themselves.
This requires a lot of technical and management training. We want the people to trust the project and feel like it's really theirs. I think it will be much easier for them to trust in it once they are fully in charge. The next big bang before we hand it over will be the screening of Markus Vetter's second film about the cinema, which will be accompanied by a symphonic orchestra performance. Internationally acclaimed musicians will come and play with Palestinian musicians during the event, and the whole thing will be transmitted live to 300 cinemas across Europe. So, lots of media attention is expected. When we have big events, we always have enough press, my concern for the cinema is to run and programme it in between the events. I don't want people here to feel like the cinema is just a platform for gathering international support.

PROJECT
PARQUE EXPLORA

ARCHITECT
**ALEJANDRO ECHEVERRI
ARQUITECTOS**

LOCATION
MEDELLÍN, COLOMBIA

View of the park at night

PARQUE EXPLORA
MEDELLÍN, COLOMBIA

PARQUE EXPLORA, THE CROWNING GLORY OF MEDELLÍN'S NEW ARCHITECTURAL AND URBAN DEVELOPMENT PLAN HELMED BY SERGIO FARJADO AND ALEJANDRO ECHEVERRI, HIGHLIGHTS EDUCATION IN THE SCIENCES WHILE STIMULATING ECONOMIC GROWTH AND TOURISM.

Parque Explora provides a multimedia interactive learning environment

CONTEXT

Over the last 20 years, neighbourhoods in Medellín have been losing status and identity due to a lack of public space and infrastructure. Social and political problems have made public building projects practically nonexistent. As a recovery strategy, a programme focusing on libraries, public buildings and parks called the 'Medellín Development Plan' was created in recent years, hoping to strengthen communities by forming new public spaces and improving educational infrastructures. The configuration of a new urban landscape is vital to the city's social transformation. In Medellín's east-central zone, an investment was made to form an integrated urban space to promote cultural activity and tourism, which manifested as the Parque Explora.

Former Medellín Mayor Sergio Fajardo and other regional officials focused particularly on the city's poorest neighbourhoods in an effort to involve the city's most disenfranchised residents.

MISSION

The Parque Explora (Exploration Park) is designed to promote free, artistic and interactive learning, with an emphasis on science and technology. Its presence supports educational institutions in the city, providing resources and space for students to expand on what they have learned in the classroom. The park hopes to impact the community at large by giving citizens a communal space and stimulating public interest in science – promoting awareness and allowing the public to make informed decisions about issues that affect them.

When the park's initial planning began in 2005, the architects started with two main questions. First of all, how could they create a museum of science and technology that would not become obsolete in the near future? And second, how could the park be structured as both a dynamic and fun place for children and an important place for adults? In order to provide answers, the team decided to depart from the traditional rigid academic conceptions of the museum, while being careful to avoid constructing an amusement park with no philosophical framework or clear purpose.

REALIZATION

The physical structure of the park addresses the natural movement and circulation of people in open spaces, as well as the relationship of the urban landscape to its natural setting – in Medellín's case, a tropical climate in a mountainous region. Parque Explora has a combination of flexible open and closed spaces that allow for constant transformation according to specific programming. Its 22,000 m2 of indoor construction and the more than 15,000 m2 of outdoor public areas are home to some 300 interactive experiences to choose from, including an aquarium, exhibition halls, an auditorium for 3D movies, a children's salon, a TV studio and themed exhibition rooms. The park as a whole is a new urban space that places emphasis on creativity, experimentation and education, allowing the population to come together as a community. Furthermore, it is a symbol of Medellín's transformation on a broad scale and the region's social and economic recovery.

—
PARQUE EXPLORA HAS A COMBINATION OF FLEXIBLE OPEN AND CLOSED SPACES THAT ALLOW FOR CONSTANT TRANSFORMATION ACCORDING TO SPECIFIC PROGRAMMING
—

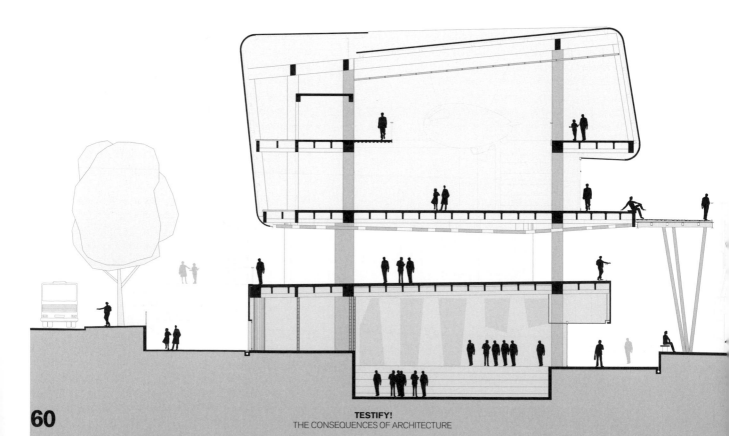

▲ The structure integrates itself with its lush natural environment

▼ A cross section of the building plan

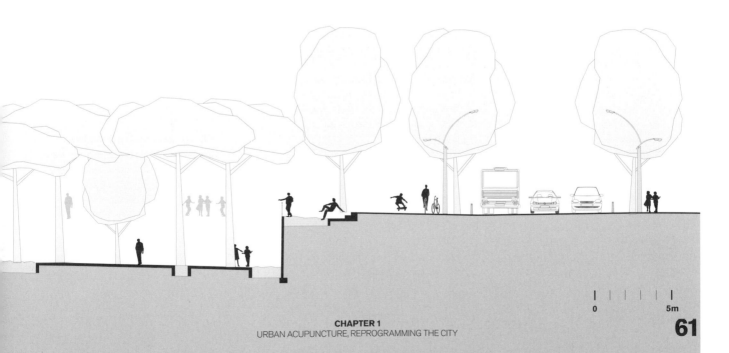

0   5m

CHAPTER 1
URBAN ACUPUNCTURE, REPROGRAMMING THE CITY

61

–
NAME
YEISON ALEXANDER HENAO

NATIONALITY
COLOMBIAN

OCCUPATION
**PROMOTER AT THE CENTRO
CULTURAL MORAVIA**

LOCATION
MEDELLÍN, COLOMBIA
–

What is the history of the area of the city where Parque Explora now stands? We are in a nationally and historically important area, because it was founded by the invasion of the people. One can still recall the landscape of slums that were built in this place, and, additionally, it is the only place in the region that had no waste treatment facilities for many years. It used to be an area with crops, crossed by the streams 'el Molino', 'la Herradura' and 'la Bermejala'. Until recently, the space that is now occupied by Parque Explora was abandoned warehouses used by the mayor's office. The train used to pass by there, and now they have conserved the old train station. In front were the botanical gardens, constructed by the city's upper class; in the 1920s they played golf and tennis there. In this zone, all kinds of opposites have coexisted. In the 1950s came the violence and, with it, the displacement of the peasants. In the midst of such poverty, influences arrived from the theology of The Liberation, the Cuban Revolution, and groups like the M19 and the ELN. Then there was the killing of leftist political groups like the Patriotic Union. Other forces like drug traffickers, paramilitary groups and various groups in conflict have also formed part of life here. Economic activities include auto mechanics and recycling – in fact, this area accounts for 60 per cent of the recycling in the entire city. There is a high rate of illiteracy, so it is very positive to have educational projects like Parque Explora.

How was the project received in the area? Was there cooperation and communication? At first the mayor's office saw us as a difficult, problematic community. The relationship improved over time. Explora created a work group with the people of the community and they had workshops, conversations . . . this made the people more positive about the project, because before that they didn't know what was going to happen in their neighbourhood.

So they talked a lot and used community input? Did they employ community workers as well? I think they all talked a lot, some things were completed, and others never got beyond hopeful plans. The people from Parque Explora conversed with the people in the neighbourhood, trying to create close relationships. I imagine that some of their ideas were taken into account. Residents were also employed in the construction zone. It was necessary to dig very deep holes for the aquarium, so many black people from the area were contracted as diggers ('moles').

And how do you see the park today? Will it continue successfully into the future? The programme is designed for the family of Moravia. The project has changed the life of the area. Before we didn't have a public space to share, to enjoy. Moreover, it has strengthened informal commerce in the park's surroundings, which has benefitted the community. The project has continued well – it's the people who use it who give it meaning.

–
NAME
ALEJANDRA NAVARRO DURÁN

NATIONALITY
COLOMBIAN

OCCUPATION
9TH GRADE STUDENT

LOCATION
MEDELLÍN, COLOMBIA
–

Are you from around here and what's your life like? Yes, I'm from Miranda. People here are not always too friendly, but my life is music – I am the daughter of a rocker, and thanks to the School of Music and the Cultural Centre, I play trumpet. I love jazz. Miles Davis is one of my favourites. I play trumpet five days a week, every afternoon.

What was in the area before the park? Do you remember its construction? It was a green area, very un-cared for, very ugly. It used to be the Botanical Gardens, with a wall around it that you couldn't see over. I don't remember anything about the construction – maybe I was too young.

What was your first thought about Parque Explora? What do you do there now? I thought they were going to put apartments or parking there. I didn't imagine that it would be such a big park with a huge aquarium. I take communications courses in the ICT room there. I finished a class on radio in which I did editing and effects . . . I loved it.

So people you know spend a lot of time there? Is it an important place? The park has a lot of life in it. In Medellín there didn't used to be any interactive learning spaces. I love to visit the Digital Projects Room, it has tons of sensors and games with music. My favourite experience there is the virtual harp.

—

'THE PARK HELPS PEOPLE UNDERSTAND THAT WE ARE NOT A BAD NEIGHBOURHOOD LIKE SOME PEOPLE SAY'

—

Do you think other things have changed in Medellín? Economically, it has had many benefits. There are places where they sell food all around the park. We love to go to the little fountains around the park, we love to get wet and throw water on people. The park helps people understand that we are not a bad neighbourhood, like some people say.

—
NAME
HAROLD GIRALDO

NATIONALITY
COLOMBIAN

OCCUPATION
BREAK DANCER

LOCATION
MEDELLÍN, COLOMBIA
—

Can you remember things before Parque Explora was built and what the construction of it was like? I remember that there used to be a lot of garbage. Everything looked very abandoned, run down, shacks and shops everywhere. Then they started moving the earth, beginning construction, and you could immediately see that they were making something. It was a tremendous project, very big – it gave us a lot to talk about. We thought that maybe they were going to build a commercial centre, a theme park, or a library.

How do you see the park? What is it for? Parque Explora is a gateway to knowledge, a place where one can find out how things work. They explain everything well. It's important that young people can get in for free.

Has the park and its programme changed things for you at all? Life has changed – you have friends in the park, you go to visit them. For

example, I go there to visit Isabel, the biologist from Parque Explora who we went to see the Amazon with. That was unforgettable. We were there for five days, and for many of us it was the first time that we had been in an airplane, or even been out of the city. We never imagined that at the end of our course on biodiversity we would get such a surprise. Those were five very happy days. We were crying when we got there. This programme changed our lives.

—

'I REMEMBER THAT THERE USED TO BE A LOT OF GARBAGE. EVERYTHING LOOKED VERY ABANDONED, RUN DOWN . . . '

—

PROJECT
LISBOA7

ARCHITECT
**AT103 / FRANCISCO PARDO
AND JULIO AMEZCUA**

LOCATION
MEXICO CITY, MEXICO

◀ Vines will eventually grow to cover several of the building's façades　　　▲ Lisboa7's interiors are all well lit with natural sunlight

Page
229 / 233

LISBOA7
MEXICO CITY, MEXICO

**A MODULAR, AFFORDABLE, AND ATTRACTIVE APARTMENT BUILDING
ADJACENT TO MEXICO CITY'S ECONOMIC CENTRE OF AVENIDA REFORMA
TAKES THE CITY A STEP CLOSER TO SOCIOECONOMIC INTEGRATION AND
THE REDUCTION OF COMMUTER TRAFFIC AND POLLUTION.**

CHAPTER 1
URBAN ACUPUNCTURE, REPROGRAMMING THE CITY

67

Geometric cut-outs make for a visually interesting living space

VARIOUS SITES LEFT EMPTY AFTER DESTRUCTION CAUSED BY EARTHQUAKES HAVE REMAINED UNDEVELOPED, AND IN SOME CASES CAN STILL BE TAKEN ADVANTAGE OF FOR RESIDENTIAL BUILDING PROJECTS

Mexico City's government started an urban renewal programme in 2003 around Avenida Reforma. It has become a main attraction in the city and the most expensive street to build on. Even so, after many of Mexico City's banks and businesses left Reforma in the last decade, the boulevard has become the centre of a real-estate renaissance.

CONTEXT

Avenida Reforma, the main avenue diagonally bisecting Mexico City, is in the midst of rapid change. Luxury apartments, retail spaces and office buildings are constantly cropping up along the avenue's skyline. The adjacent blocks in each neighbourhood are likewise affected by these new developments, quickly becoming service areas for this new commercial centre. Lower-income workers who have jobs near Reforma but cannot afford to live in the area must make long daily commutes, contributing to the city's already serious problems of congestion and pollution.

MISSION

In order to avoid massive gentrification along Reforma and its surrounding areas, Francisco Pardo and at 103 s.c. realized the need for low- and middle-income housing to counter-balance Reforma's developments. Various sites left empty after destruction caused by earthquakes have remained undeveloped, and in some cases can still be taken advantage of for residential building projects.

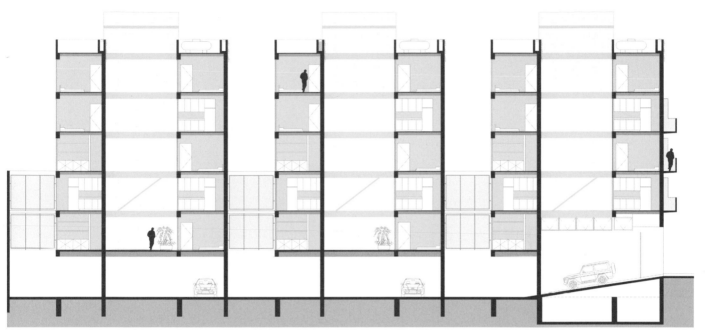

This diagram reveals the building's underground garage

These blocks need to be considered carefully in order to help the area serve as a symbiotic system; new housing should not compete with existing structures, but become part of the area's social fabric. The architects also believe that it is important that the housing be able to gain value over time, making it good investment property. Unlike much of Mexico City's housing, Lisboa7 intends to maximize space and efficiency while still allowing a decent quality of life.

REALIZATION

The architects developed a dense building that was spatially designed by dividing the maximum density allowed for housing in Mexico into six volumes. The building has 60 modules overall, each measuring 36 m2, which is the minimum area permissible in Mexico. The building has five levels with only two corridors, which run along the second and fourth floors. Individual units are laid out differently and some are interconnected to allow larger spaces for families. However, larger units take up more vertical, not horizontal space, ranging from one to three levels – this makes them feel more like small houses than apartments.

Each module has a free plan and a service area for either a kitchen or a bathroom that can be programmed as needed. One aspect of the spatial design is therefore largely left up to inhabitants. Basic construction materials have been used – cinder block and exposed concrete – and are generally left unfinished.

All the living spaces face west; the east side is almost entirely closed to provide privacy between the units. When working with dense housing, the quality of the spaces is very important, so Lisboa7 units have good natural light, ventilation and outdoor views where possible. A vertical garden runs along the eastern façades.

architecture around here. The building itself appears to me in harmony with the style of the architecture preceding it in the neighbourhood, but it shows an attitude of renewal, which lends new value to its neighbours. It also maintains a proper balance between security and convenience, and it has an intelligent spatial distribution plan that allows for easy maintenance. Although this is an old part of the city, it's constantly in restoration.

–
OCCUPANTS
A COUPLE AND ONE 3-YEAR-OLD CHILD

OCCUPATION
CLERK AND NURSE

APPARTMENT
A4

NUMBER OF MODULES
TWO
–

What is the area you are living in like? Lisboa 7 is in a zone close to one of biggest avenues and the city's commercial district. There's a lot of movement on weekdays – pedestrians and cars, people going to work at offices and businesses on the street. And we regularly feel the effect of strikes in the city, due to its proximity to numerous governmental buildings, embassies and the Mexican stock exchange. Reforma has become a traditional place for Mexicans to celebrate or protest. Most protest rallies commonly go along Reforma. During the weekend, things are much calmer. There are plenty of parks to visit and things to do with my family on the weekends.

What made you move into this building? My wife works nearby. Even though I travel a bit farther for my job, it's okay, since I like living here. Also because I believe that we will witness an economic growth in this area. It seems like an attempt is being made to remodel a lot of the

–
OCCUPANTS
ONE MALE ADULT AND TWO GIRLS (7 AND 9 YEARS OLD)

OCCUPATION
DESIGNER

APPARTMENT
B2

NUMBER OF MODULES
THREE
–

What was the state of the site before the building was erected and what's daily life like around here? As far as I know it was just a lot, left empty since the 1985 earthquake and used for parking. This is a very old neighbourhood that was damaged pretty badly during the earthquake. It's a strange area as it is at the very centre of the city close to the Paseo de la Reforma, one of Mexico City's largest boulevards cutting diagonally

–
'IT'S VERY LIVELY DURING THE WEEKDAYS AND BUSINESS HOURS BUT IT FEELS RATHER ABANDONED AT NIGHT AND ON THE WEEKENDS'
–

across the entire city. Many monuments to people and events in Mexico's history are situated on and along Reforma as well as lots of restaurants and hotels and office buildings and new construction around here. So, it's very lively during the weekdays and business hours but it feels rather abandoned at night and on the weekends.

How is the area changing?
The back end of Reforma where this building is located will probably change a lot in the next five to ten years. As I said, up until now it's still a rather business-oriented neighbourhood with few residential buildings, but as more and more people prefer to not commute from the suburbs every day, they will move back into the centre again. More density of population will do this area good. What I really like about living here in general and in particular in this building, is the fact that it somehow manages to close off the city's chaos from you and gives you a sense of privacy and seclusion, even though you are right in the middle of everything here as soon as you step out of the house.

–
OCCUPANTS
ONE ADULT MALE

OCCUPATION
BANKER

APPARTMENT
B3

NUMBER OF MODULES
TWO
–

How do you see this typical commercial city centre change in the future?
There are a lot of buildings being built on Reforma, and this will bring money and services to the area. I also think that slowly, some of the abandoned buildings will be refurbished and the whole area will change for better and that the value of buildings in this neighbourhood will increase considerably in the future. There is a new tendency towards living in the city centre rather than living in the suburbs. My quality of life has increased since I can now walk to work instead of commuting for two hours a day in this city's terrible traffic. But this area still needs some time to be accepted as a residential area. Now there are just a few apartment buildings in this neighbourhood, mostly just small services like shops and restaurants and the big offices on Reforma. Nearby, there are also still some shops that sell illegal car parts, which is a bad image for the neighbourhood. I guess that is the reason why not very many people want to live around here.

–
OCCUPANTS
**TWO ADULTS AND ONE CHILD
(7 YEARS OLD)**

OCCUPATION
ARCHITECT

APPARTMENT
B7

NUMBER OF MODULES
FOUR
–

Do you see this building as part of a larger change in this part of Mexico City?
The whole Avenida Reforma has changed dramatically in the last years; new buildings house offices that employ thousands of people. These people want to live closer to their jobs, so the surrounding neighbourhoods are developing housing for this need, especially middle-income housing.

How does the building integrate itself in the surrounding neighbourhood?
This area is characterized by a mix of contemporary styles and the commonly used style for office blocks. There are also very few of the original nineteenth-century houses built in different European architectural styles left. Against this backdrop, this building keeps a rather low-key appearance. It not so flashy and it gives us a lot of privacy. You never know if a neighbour is inside or not. I really like the way the architect left the façades, just cinder block, exposed. It will age

nicely without any maintenance costs, and it will look great in the future when all the vines grow over it. I always tell my friends who visit that the building is like a baby that will grow into maturity, always looking good.

Has the project been well-received by community members?
I think that most people around here see the building as a good thing for the area. Instead of having an empty lot with cars, you have 24 hours of activity in the street. Having 19 new families moving here will bring more activity to the street and local businesses. It's just a little piece, but you see this kind of building more and more – the area will be great in a few years.

–
'THE BUILDING KEEPS A RATHER LOW-KEY APPEARANCE. ITS NOT SO FLASHY AND GIVES US A LOT OF PRIVACY'
–

PROJECT
ENERGY NEUTRAL MONUMENT

ARCHITECT
ZECC ARCHITECTEN

LOCATION
**DRIEBERGEN-UTRECHT,
THE NETHERLANDS**

ENERGY NEUTRAL MONUMENT DRIEBERGEN
DRIEBERGEN-UTRECHT, THE NETHERLANDS

ZECC ARCHITECTEN SUCCESSFULLY RENOVATED A HISTORICAL MONUMENT IN DRIEBERGEN TO BE COMPLETELY ENERGY-NEUTRAL, FULFILLING BOTH THE REQUIREMENTS FOR HISTORICAL PRESERVATION AND THE STANDARDS FOR ENERGY EFFICIENCY. THE ATTRACTIVE HOUSE, ALL OF WHOSE RENOVATIONS ARE IN FACT REVERSIBLE, IS CURRENTLY LIVED IN, AND ITS PLANNING PROCESS IS AN EXAMPLE FOR COUNTLESS FUTURE INITIATIVES OF ITS KIND.

All changes to the historic architecture are reversible

CONTEXT

The villa in Driebergen is a monument from the beginning of the twentieth century; inside the villa, time has stood still. The house seems mysterious from the outside, owing to the large, dark trees in the backyard and its unkempt façade. Inside, all the original elements are present and in good condition. Only a thin layer of paint covers the wooden frames and profiling. Old glass ventilation slats provide plenty of fresh air. The owners bought the villa from the municipality because they had the progressive idea to transform the monument into a zero-energy house. Together with OPAI, a plan was created to realize the first energy-neutral monument in the Netherlands: a house that provides its own energy via high-quality systems. Zecc Architects integrated the energy concept in the existing monument and adjusted the villa to the wishes of its future residents.

Given the fact that our built environment is in most parts of the world still largely determined by existing buildings and structures rather than by new developments, one of the great challenges for today's architects is the creative handling and inspiring transformation of such architectural remains.

MISSION

Zecc is experienced in the restoration of monuments and reuse of cultural heritage. In previous years, the architects have worked primarily with two objectives: first, to preserve the monument, and second, to give it a new life through a contemporary adaptation or addition. With the villa in Driebergen, the vision was enriched by a third objective: to make the monument energy-ready for the future. There is no standard recipe for this transformation. For each monument, a new balance has to be found between an energy concept and the monumentality of the building. Careful considerations have to be made as far as the choice of materials and accommodating the inhabitants' needs.

REALIZATION

Many groups of people worked closely together to fulfil this project, due to the complexity of its ambition. A working conference was organized in close cooperation with the community, during which the many viewpoints and multiplicity of interests involved became visible. During the integrated design process, the priority to create an energy-neutral monument served at each phase as a benchmark from which the next steps could be made. The fact that people were able to come together to come up with new solutions and share knowledge in an open planning process is seen as this project's most important factor of success. Geothermal energy for the house is harnessed using a heat pump, a buffer barrel and ground collectors. The house is heated by floor and wall heating and hot water is made with a heat pump boiler. The electricity needed for the heat pump is obtained from PV solar panels on the roof of the main house and the new extension at its back. On sunny days, this energy is supplied to the public network, and on dark days energy is extracted from the public network. The entirety is energy neutral, but the house stays continuously connected to the public electricity network. The monument committee objected to solar panels on the rear roof of the villa, but this had to be done to make a truly neutral monument. Fortunately, the panels are completely out of sight, and together with the panels on the roof of the new extension, enough energy for the house is provided. To reduce heat loss, the house is insulated with sustainable materials: the wooden roof, for instance, is insulated with flax, a breathable and sustainable material that prevents condensation.

The owners wanted a large kitchen and light dining room overlooking the garden. These functions were fulfilled in the new extension built at the back of the house. The structure now progresses from traditional at the front to modern at the back. The finish of the new façades is plaster with crushed bricks from the demolished previous extension, incorporating a physical part of the building's history in its new construction. By making the conversion glazing on the house bigger than the old wooden frames, a part of the masonry from the original façade remains visible. The new insulation layer is kept visually separate from the monument. The architects paid a lot of attention to retaining the structure's original detail, and made interventions that were essentially reversible. Moreover, the additions are readable in the different building layers, making history visible via architectural stratification.

▼ An entirely energy-neutral living space

▶ The new façade still exposes historic details

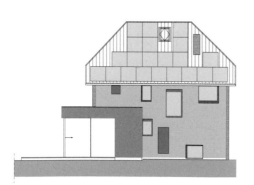

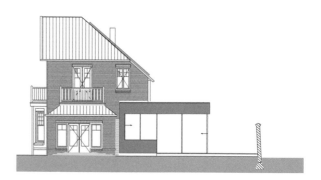

–
NAME
LIESBETH WASSENBERG

NATIONALITY
DUTCH

OCCUPATION
**ENERGY NEUTRAL MONUMENT
PROJECT MANAGER**

LOCATION
UTRECHT, THE NETHERLANDS
–

When did you decide to buy the house? How did the plan get started? The municipality owned the house and decided to sell it after the previous tenant passed away in 2008, in a contest on the criteria of sustainability and price. First we contacted One Planet Architecture institute, the knowledge centre of RAU architects who designed the concept for an energy neutral monument. After winning the bid, we contacted Zecc Architects to translate the concept into an architectural design, balancing the building's important heritage with a sustainable energy concept.

How did the design process work? The design was made by the architect and adjusted in dialogue with the local heritage committee and the buyer. The design barely changed at all during construction. For the renovation, natural (and sustainable) materials were used, like flax, hemp, clay, recycled glass and green concrete paint based on linseed oil. No chemical materials like gypsum

or polyurethane were used. Most labourers worked for a local contractor, but also a clay worker from Germany helped out.

Are you currently living in the house? Have you changed anything? We have been living in the house since October 2010. No modifications have been made, and I hope we will not have to make them in the coming years. The architects are still in touch; they publish about the project, and together we organize conferences and give lectures about it. A lot of people are interested. We've founded a foundation for the sustainable renovation of historical buildings that shares knowledge through websites and a LinkedIn group on the Internet. Yet we are still fine tuning. The house should be self-sustaining (for heating and hot water) but the installation is being modified to reach this goal. The project has drawn a lot of attention locally and nationally. A lot of people still pause by the house to look at it. People are happy that the house has regained its quality and like the realization of the sustainable possibilities.

Has the project impacted the community in a larger sense? Beyond its physical presence, have the project and the process had wider effects on the area's residents? No, not the house itself. But as the first energy-neutral monument in the Netherlands, it is an inspiration and an example that there are a lot of possibilities for sustainable renovation – even for historic buildings and monuments.

–
NAME
**MARIETJE VAN EEGHEN
AND ARNO DE GEEST**

NATIONALITY
DUTCH

OCCUPATION
**ENVIRONMENTAL ADVISER
AND RESTORATION ADVISER**

LOCATION
UTRECHT, THE NETHERLANDS
–

Let's start at the beginning. How did you get involved in the project in the first place? *Arno:* I got involved when the city council decided to sell this house, which has a special historical status as a monument.

Marietje: Yes, this house was owned by the city council and when it was put up for sale, we decided to include the sustainability issue in the selling process. People who were interested in buying the house had to offer a certain amount of money, but they also had to offer a plan on how they would renovate the building. The people who finally bought the house had come up with the best plan. It was very ambitious to make a historical monument entirely energy neutral. In our area, there are several villages with lots of monuments and nice old buildings, and it's also very green – so sustainability and monumental value were already two big issues in our community. So we thought this would be a very good opportunity to see how far we could go with this energy neutral ambition.

How did the architects actually get involved? Were they part of the original plan that the buyers had submitted? *Marietje:* Initially, when the buyers submitted their plan for the renovation, the architect was not involved yet. There was another organization who first contributed to the energy concept of the renovation of the house. The next step was to contract the architect, and after the architect made a plan we had a big meeting with a lot of experts.

Arno: We had local and national experts at this meeting, trying to find the best solutions for many problems.

Marietje: Yes, there were many practical problems: How could we conserve the nice details of the monument while at the same time insulating the house and installing devices to generate energy? There were some pretty big dilemmas in finding a way to preserve and respect the monument, and at the same time trying to meet this very high ambition of making it energy neutral.

So it was a comprehensive look at the whole building with two priorities, trying to balance both of them against each other. *Marietje:* Right. And it was really a process of getting those two worlds together and finding out step-by-step what we could do and what was the best way to go about it.

Arno: It wasn't easy. Those worlds speak different languages. The best way was to try to find a general goal and then work from there.

Marietje: The architects really had to manoeuvre between those two worlds, and stay in very close contact and discuss things, to bring them together. And well, they did do a very good job.

Arno: A very good job. I think they were one of the best architects to solve this kind of problem. They were always in contact with the other specialists. It was a struggle for the best solution, though. Every detail was discussed.

How did it work with the city government? Since the house takes energy from the public supply and then gives it back when there is a surplus? *Marietje:* That's a rather technical question. There are solar panels and a heating system on the highest part of the roof. On days when there is a surplus, the electricity goes back into the main system, and on days when there is not enough, the opposite happens. But that is an issue for the energy supplier, which is a private company. The main issue for the government was whether or not we were compromising our standards for maintaining a monument by making the house very sustainable. That was the struggle we had.

How did it end up so successfully? Was that related to the fact that the architect was around so much, present and engaged in the discussion? *Arno:* Absolutely, it was necessary to have an architect who understands both of those worlds, and who could connect them – getting people together and discussing things in detail.

The way of dealing with monuments is very traditional; those people are not readily going to accept new materials or philosophies. They use what they know, which is a problem – if you want to make progress, then you have to try something new. In the end, the result is good for everyone.

It probably changes everybody's outlook a bit for the next projects. Speaking of next projects: what could happen next? What are your plans? *Marietje:* Well, there are

some things that are perhaps on their way . . . and we will certainly use the lessons that we learned from this project.

Arno: We hope that there will be very good architects working with the new plans again, as it really proved that the architect is the centre of the project. They have to be able to translate the requirements and the ambitions of both worlds into a house, into a plan. But, it's not possible to copy what we did with this house when working with other buildings. You have to have the whole struggle again. You can't make a quick copy – it doesn't work that way.

Marietje: Yes, I think that's right. If you copy something, you should copy the process, not the specifics of the technical renovation, but perhaps it's the process

Arno: Copy the process! Not the outcome. You have to do the project again each time, with good professionals who understand their jobs.

—

'THERE WERE SOME PRETTY BIG DILEMMAS IN FINDING A WAY TO RESPECT THE MONUMENT, AND AT THE SAME TIME TRYING TO MAKE IT ENERGY NEUTRAL'

—

SMOOTH OPERATORS

—

INTERVENTIONS
IN THE PUBLIC REALM

PROJECT
BOGOTÁ CHANGE

CREATOR
**ANTANAS MOCKUS AND
ENRIQUE PEÑALOSA**

LOCATION
BOGOTÁ, COLOMBIA

Mayor Peñalosa reconstructed an enormous part of Bogotá during his term

BOGOTÁ CHANGE
BOGOTÁ, COLOMBIA

**TWO MAYORS HAVE COMPLETELY TRANSFORMED THE CULTURAL
CLIMATE AND PHYSICAL LANDSCAPE OF COLOMBIA'S CAPITAL CITY,
LONG CONSIDERED ONE OF THE MOST DANGEROUS CITIES ON THE PLANET;
ONE MAYOR THROUGH OFTEN-DRAMATIC AND HILARIOUS PUBLIC
INTERVENTIONS, THE OTHER THROUGH DRASTIC STRUCTURAL
AND INFRASTRUCTURAL RENOVATIONS.**

The city's streets used to be extremely dangerous for pedestrians and bicycle riders

CONTEXT

In the early 1990s, Colombia's capital Bogotá was considered one of the most violent cities in the world. The nation as a whole had a 20 per cent unemployment rate, and 55 per cent of the Colombians lived below the poverty line. Declining exports, political instability and widespread urbanization had lead to a proliferation of slums in Bogotá, many of which lacked basic services. Because the growth was unplanned, urban areas suffered from inadequate means of disposing of wastewater, severe groundwater pollution, water shortages and traffic congestion as people commute daily from the periphery to the centre. The country's natural environment was threatened by deforestation, pesticide use and air pollution – particularly in the capital.

According to Bourdieu, symbolic violence reveals the dynamics of power relations in social life. As for all of his investigative frameworks and terminologies, symbolic violence emphasizes the role of practice and embodiment or forms in social dynamics and worldview construction.

MISSION

Antanas Mockus was a long-time professor and researcher at the National University of Colombia, and served both as its vice president (1988-1991) and its president (1991-1993). As its president, he contributed to the formulation of the Colombian Constitution of 1991, focusing on educational issues. In a notable 1993 incident, when confronted with a disruptive group of students, he mooned them. He later explained his action by saying 'Innovative behaviour can be useful when you run out of words', and linked it to philosopher Pierre Bourdieu's concept of 'symbolic violence'.

In 1993, riding a wave of publicity from his mooning scandal, Mockus ran for mayor of Bogotá and won. Under his leadership the city saw improvements: water usage dropped 40 per cent, 7,000 community security groups were formed and the homicide rate fell 70 per cent, traffic fatalities dropped by over 50 per cent, drinking water was provided to all homes (up from 79 per cent in 1993), and sewerage was provided to 95 per cent of homes (up from 71 per cent). When he asked residents to pay a voluntary extra 10 per cent in taxes, 63,000 people did so. One of his famous initiatives was to hire 420 mimes to make fun of traffic violators, because he believed Colombians were more afraid of being ridiculed than fined. He also initiated a 'Women's Night', on which the city's men were asked to stay home for an evening to look after the house and the children. His initiatives to reduce violence by engaging citizens in civil resistance were both original and successful. During his second term as mayor, beginning in 2001, he successfully combined showmanship, fiscal discipline and heavy reliance on punitive measures.

Enrique Peñalosa governed Bogotá in the three-year period between Mockus's two stints. Peñalosa inherited his interest in urban issues from his father, a one-time Bogotá City Council member and housing specialist for the United Nations. When Peñalosa took office, he launched a near-obsessive crusade to reform the city's public transport system. Peñalosa declared a virtual War on Cars, restricting traffic during peak hours to reduce rush hour traffic by 40 per cent and convincing the City Council to increase the tax on gasoline. Half of the revenues generated by the increase were then poured into a bus system that currently serves 500,000 Bogotá residents every day. 'We had to build a city not for businesses or automobiles, but for children and thus for people,' Peñalosa said. 'Instead of building highways, we restricted car use. We invested in high-quality sidewalks, pedestrian streets, parks, bicycle paths, libraries; we got rid of thousands of cluttering commercial signs and planted trees. All our everyday efforts have one objective: Happiness.'

While Peñalosa has been credited with the physical changes, Mockus's stunts won much of the population over, reinvesting Bogotá's citizens with a certain amount of trust in their government. Much of Peñalosa's drastic urban remodelling would not have been possible if Mockus's public antics had not begun to cause a cultural shift. During Mockus's first term, he strolled the streets in red and blue tights as a 'Super Citizen', giving tips on civility. He starred in a televised public service announcement to promote water conservation – while in the shower. He ran his last campaign on a platform composed almost entirely of traffic issues, has exhorted city residents to 'arm themselves with love', and has been credited with doing away with corrupt police officers. These funny and provocative acts of public intervention changed the city's political climate, and were in part what paved the way for Peñalosa's virtual transformation of the urban landscape in an incredibly short three years.

WHEN PEÑALOSA TOOK OFFICE, HE LAUNCHED A NEAR-OBSESSIVE CRUSADE TO REFORM THE CITY'S PUBLIC TRANSPORT SYSTEM

REALIZATION

According to the New York Times, Bogotá is now safer than Caracas, Rio de Janiero, Washington, DC, and Baltimore. In 2000, Peñalosa was honoured with the Stockholm Challenge Award for creating Bogotá's car-free day – the largest and most successful event of its kind in the world. The award focused significant international attention on Bogotá and caused the United Nations, in partnership with a variety of other organizations, to organize a workshop in Bogotá for other mayors interested in creating car-free days in their cities. Mockus is currently the president of Corpovisionarios, an organization that provides consulting services to cities about addressing their problems through the same policy methodology that was so successful during his terms as mayor of Bogotá. In 2010, he ran for president of Colombia with the recently-formed Green Party, losing by 27.5 per cent of the vote.

The impact of Mockus and Peñalosa on the development of Bogotá is described in a documentary film released in October 2009 called Cities on Speed – Bogotá Change. It is promoted as being 'the story of two charismatic mayors, Antanas Mockus and Enrique Peñalosa who, with unorthodox methods, in less than ten years turned one of the world's most dangerous, violent and corrupt capitals into a peaceful model city populated by caring citizens'. With Mockus and Peñalosa and key members of their staff as firsthand witnesses, the film uncovers the ideas, philosophies and strategies that underlie the changes in Bogotá and are now being exported to cities worldwide.

▶ The city's streets used to be extremely dangerous for pedestrians and bicycle riders

'I REMEMBER HOW THINGS WERE BEFORE EITHER MOCKUS OR PEÑALOSA WAS ELECTED. THE TWO MAYORS UNDOUBTEDLY CHANGED THE QUALITY OF LIFE OF BOGOTÁ'S INHABITANTS AND VISITORS'

NAME
MARCELA AGUILAR

NATIONALITY
COLOMBIAN

OCCUPATION
DENTIST

LOCATION
BOGOTÁ, COLOMBIA

Do you remember daily life in Bogotá before either Mockus or Peñalosa was in office?
I remember how things were before either Mockus or Peñalosa was elected. The two mayors undoubtedly changed the quality of life of Bogotá's inhabitants and visitors. Before their terms as mayor, it was not possible to walk along the sidewalks in many streets; one had to walk in the street. Chaos and insecurity reigned in the city.

Can you recall any anecdotes about encounters with their projects? Well, I do remember Mockus's symbolic interventions as mayor! In order to fight the appalling number of pedestrian deaths in Bogotá, for example, he hired street mimes to mimic people who continued to break traffic and jaywalking rules, asserting that Colombians were more afraid of being humiliated than fined. The mimes followed the unlucky offenders, taunting them and flashing signs that said 'INCORRECTO' when they broke the rules. During Mockus's terms, traffic deaths dropped by more than 50 per cent due to this and other interventions.

Later Mockus said that it was a pacifist counterweight. With neither words nor weapons, the mimes were doubly unarmed. His goal was to show the importance of cultural regulations. Later the city painted yellow outlined stars on the exact locations where 1500 pedestrians were killed by cars. Some busy intersections were covered with the stars, forming constellations on the asphalt.

What is your impression of the large-scale changes that occurred in the city during the 1990s?
Today, one can travel on the pedestrian walkways, which are wide and calm. Unfortunately, the last two mayors have given up public space, again giving it to informal vendors. I use the Transmilenio bus system, which was inaugurated by Peñalosa, twice a week. The public transport system has improved considerably, but it is still insufficient for the number of people who want to use it, and congestion is becoming a problem. Mockus and Peñalosa changed the city positively, but the most recent mayors in office have brought chaos back.

NAME
ADRIANA TORRES TOPAGA

NATIONALITY
COLOMBIAN

OCCUPATION
DESIGNER/ARTIST

LOCATION
LINZ, AUSTRIA
–

Do you remember when either Mockus or Peñalosa was mayor? What is your impression of the effect they had on the city? In my experience, the result of Mockus's tactics was a change of attitude, a surging of a new sense of belonging. Many things changed, but the important result was really the relationship of the inhabitants to their city. Before Mockus, people from Bogotá complained all the time about the city, but after his term as mayor, despite the continued infrastructure failures, the spirit of Bogotá had changed in favour of the desire for a better city and a certain 'civic consciousness'. I should mention that I only lived in Bogotá until 1996, during Mockus's first term as mayor.

Do you have specific memories of any of Mockus's initiatives?
I remember various initiatives and symbolic interventions such as the 'Las estrellas negras' (The black stars), when he painted yellow outlined black stars throughout the city on the exact locations where 1500 pedestrians were killed by cars. Some busy intersections were covered with the stars, forming constellations on the asphalt. Then naturally his 'La Hora Zanahoria' (The Carrot Hour). In Colombian collo-

quialisms, a zanahoria is someone who neither drinks nor smokes and lives healthily. Driven by his deep conviction that all life is sacred, Mockus tackled driving fatalities on weekends by introducing the so called carrot law, which forced Bogotá's nightspots to close at 1 a.m. While the law was not initially popular, it was hard to argue with the results. Weekend traffic fatalities fell from 16 to just four. From 'La Hora Zanahoria', I especially remember the dramatic change in the weekends, when parties started earlier, and the next day everyone had more energy than on the regular schedule.

How do you distinguish between the two mayors? How do you imagine their respective roles?
The two mayors had a complementary relationship. The first changed the city's attitude, and the second continued with these ideas, bringing to fruition necessary infrastructural changes. I think that a certain mutual respect and recognition exists between the two politicians, which was visible during the 2010 presidential elections when the two former mayors, along with a third former mayor named Lucho Garzón, ran for president as one candidate, backed by the Green Party.

—

'THE FIRST MAYOR CHANGED THE CITY'S ATTITUDE, AND THE SECOND CONTINUED WITH THESE IDEAS, BRINGING TO FRUITION NECESSARY INFRASTRUCTURAL CHANGES'

—

PROJECT
ESTONOESUNSOLAR

ARCHITECT
**GRÁVALOS DI MONTE
ARQUITECTOS**

LOCATION
ZARAGOZA, SPAIN

Reclaiming abandoned urban plots has provided space for community use

Page
7 / 229 /
233

ESTONOESUNSOLAR
ZARAGOZA, SPAIN

THROUGH A SERIES OF URBAN INTERVENTIONS, THE ESTONOESUNSOLAR PROGRAMME CREATED USABLE SPACES OUT OF ABANDONED VACANT LOTS IN THE CITY OF ZARAGOZA. THE LOW-COST PROJECT SHOWS HOW SMALL CHANGES CAN TRANSFORM THE CITY LANDSCAPE THROUGH IMAGINATION AND COMMUNITY INVOLVEMENT.

Low-cost interventions can have a huge community impact

CONTEXT

Numerous urban plots lie entirely unused and vacant in Zaragoza's historical centre. The demolition of old structures has exposed a new type of urban space. The initial objective of the 'estonoesunsolar' (this is not an empty urban plot) programme was based on an employment plan in which 61 people who had long been unemployed were paid to clean up the empty plots of Zaragoza's historical district. This programme provided Patrizia Di Monte and Ignacio Grávalos Lacambra with the opportunity to experiment with a new type of temporary urban intervention. Their creative ideas for the reuse of empty space originated in the 'Vacíos Cotidianos' (Empty everyday places) programme, which took place within the framework of the 2006 'En La Frontera' urban art festival in Zaragoza. During this festival, the project creators were able to begin testing their ideas about temporary occupation, in this case in a strictly 'artistic' context. These experiments were then expanded upon during a two-year endeavour.
The 'estonoesunsolar' programme gathered the proposals of two architects and several associations and neighbourhood organizations, channelling institutional support for the projects' completion.

The celebration of the perennial interim solution here becomes the status quo, transforming the city into an open laboratory and propagating its experimental spirit.

MISSION

The richness of possibilities to use the empty urban plots stems from the indeterminacy of such gaps in the regular urban fabric. Temporary interventions in the city space are a dynamic tool that allow for flexible, alternative readings of the city. The project as a whole aims for non-material solutions, establishing an open dialogue with the constructed environment through a light-hearted attitude. From the outset, it was essential to find a name for the interventions that gave meaning to a programme without a programme, an owner without property, an urban plot without a building, a place with no name. The name 'estonoesunsolar' was intended to propose a new way of seeing familiar places: this is not an empty place – this is not what it seems. In short, it is an invitation to think again, to imagine possibilities, to propose new situations and create enthusiastic spaces. Among the numerous games and creative processes at work throughout the process, the underlying goal was to revitalize the vast overlooked urban areas, encouraging the public to see empty space as an opportunity, not a sign of neglect.

▲ Lighting unused areas at night increases safety and accessibility

▶ Parts of Zargoza are now more bike- and child-friendly

REALIZATION

All the ideas for the project eventually crystallized into concrete interventions. There were two distinct periods in which the interventions took place: from July to December 2009, and from June to December 2010. The project, while always focusing on the same basic goals, had a very different character during these two blocks of time. The proceedings of 2009, framed exclusively in the field of historical Zaragoza, had a very small scale, but the interventions were coherent as a single body of work due to their proximity and thematic regularity. The interventions took place mainly in the districts of San Pablo, Magdalena and Arrabal, and the projects ranged from planting an urban garden, bowling in the street and constructing giant board games to holding an open call for classes from public schools to propose a use for the empty space. A jury consisting of journalists and architects selected and executed the winning proposal, a park with illuminated trees and benches entitled 'Theater of Luck'.

Given the success of the 2009 projects, the Zaragoza City Council decided to extend estonoesunsolar's projects to other districts of the city. Taking what had

At the recent 11th Spanish Architecture and Urbanism Biennial 2011, Grávalos di Monte Arquitectos received the Research Award for the estonoesunsolar project.

been learned during the previous year, in 2010 many new projects were initiated, including building a walkway over the Ebro River, building playgrounds, parks and basketball courts, installing hanging lighting systems, planting olive trees and creating a 'memory park' simulating the mechanism of memory for Alzheimer's patients. Lastly, estonoesunsolar organized a series of outdoor movie screenings on the historical plots. Plots were chosen in the neighbourhoods of San Pablo and the Magdalena, which are at opposite ends of the district from each other, reiterating the emphasis on the integration of a large area and interaction. The projects are each so varied, complex and specifically related to the conditions of their immediate environments that an overview does not do them justice. In each project, however, collaboration with the local citizens was the most important driving factor. Much effort has been invested in sharing the experience with other cities through lectures and publications. The programme has attracted the interest of professional groups, university settings and public institutions, and has received numerous recognitions and awards.

–
NAME
AMELIA HERNÁNDEZ CAUSAPÉ

NATIONALITY
SPANISH

OCCUPATION
PERFORMING ARTIST

LOCATION
ZARAGOZA, SPAIN
–

Some of the spaces that form part of the estoesunsolar project were created in the old part of the city of Zaragoza. What is the area like? The old town of Zaragoza is the second largest historical district in Spain. The current population is multicultural, and the different cultures generally coexist in a positive way. This coexistence of life is reflected on the street. Many small businesses owned by immigrants are flourishing, and young artists and designers have begun new businesses as well. The old town is a popular leisure area for people who live in other parts of the city, who come principally there for the cafés, restaurants and shops. Tourists are also common in the old town, because most of the city's important monuments and museums are in the area. One of the greatest shortcomings in this part of the city is the lack of open public space. Most of the buildings are old and generally don't exceed four storeys. Many have been renovated, and others are in the rehabilitation process.

Some have been torn down because they have deteriorated too much. Sometimes brand-new buildings are built, but often vacant lots are left indefinitely after demolition. These empty spaces, which are usually fenced off, gradually deteriorate and create an image of abandonment, neglect, and unsafety. Some of these empty places are only temporarily unused, and some have become permanently abandoned.

How did the estoesunsolar project address these empty spaces? This was an innovative project, which has created affordable and useful solutions for vacant public and private space through design and creativity. The project aims to create a new mode for public use, integrating the vacant lots with their environment and with the needs of the people in this area. To determine what these needs were, the architects collaborated with the local associations in each area, who were invited to submit proposals. Public participation was actively sought out. One of the most interesting projects, which happened near where I live, was

—
'THE KIDS IN THE OLD TOWN WERE INVITED TO PARTICIPATE IN DESIGNING THE FUTURE PLAN OF ONE OF THE EMPTY LOTS'
—

carried out with children. The kids in the old town were invited to participate in designing the future plan of one of the empty lots. Working in 15 groups for two days with the architects, they made scale models of their proposals for the space. One of the proposals was selected and it was built. For all of the children, it was an enriching and unforgettable experience.

Who was employed for construction and where did the materials come from? Workers with a long-term history of unemployment were hired for the project. In fact, the majority of the project budget was used to recruit and pay staff. I attended the openings of several of the projects, and I saw that workers who had participated in the construction were there at the events – some had even brought their families! I think the materials used are mostly local and recycled; the project had a very low cost per square metre.

How have the spaces been used since the opening days? The spaces are currently in good condition. The project was received well in the community – it was a wonderful surprise. There are new places for children, sports areas, small plazas, gardens … neighbourhood groups are bound to maintain these new places. It is hoped that the residents will make the project self-sustaining – only time will tell. We hope so! The project has graced and dignified many streets just by its physical presence. The architects achieved their goals in creating versatile spaces that can be utilized for lots of things – they are places for coexistence and enjoyment – truly free spaces. Recently, they just opened a temporary art exhibition with three local artists in an abandoned site – street art! I love it! It's the best way to reach the citizens!

—
NAME
BELINDA MARTÍNEZ OSTALÉ

NATIONALITY
SPANISH

OCCUPATION
**EDUCATOR. PRESIDENT OF THE OS
MESACHES RECREATION CENTRE AND
EDUCATOR AT THE OS MESACHES
CHILDREN'S CENTRE**

LOCATION
ZARAGOZA, SPAIN
—

—

'THE PROJECT HAS BEEN A SMALL REVOLUTION FOR THE AREA – IT NOT ONLY PHYSICALLY IMPROVED THE ENVIRONMENT BY ELIMINATING A NEGLECTED AND DIRTY SPOT, BUT IT ALSO CREATED A PLACE FOR PEOPLE OF ALL AGES TO COME TOGETHER'

—

How did the project arise? How was initial contact with the architects made? The Os Mesaches recreation centre, where I work, tried to reclaim the plot years ago, proposing to pave over the space with asphalt in order to eliminate the waste problem and create a square for the local residents to use. But this initiative was not successful. In the summer of 2010, the Zaragoza City Council, under the governance of the United Left party, got in touch with our association in the hopes of reclaiming the empty plot as part of the esto-noesunsolar programme. We gladly accepted.

How did the process unfold? How was a use for the space determined? After several meetings, the Os Mesaches centre decided to organize workshops with local children in order to design a space together. In the workshops, they made drawings, models and even real-size representa-tions of their ideas on the ground of the new space. In one workshop with their parents, the kids and neighbours presented their finished works.

Has the project been well-received by community members? How do they use it and how do they treat the space? The lot is always busy with children, youths and adults of any age. Lots of people come to play basketball – some are on federal teams, some come from other neighbourhood associations, and some are just local people playing together. People even come on weekday mornings. Parents come with their children to play football or basketball, to skate, play with toys, whatever. The users of the recreation centre finally have a safe and versatile place to play outdoors. Everyone, without exception, respects the space. It stays clean and free of vandalism. The project has kept itself alive. It has been accepted enormously well by people of all ages.

It is respected by the residents and has not suffered any damage.

How has the project impacted the community in a larger sense? The project has been a small revolution for the area – it not only physically improved the environment by eliminating a neglected and dirty spot, but it also created a place for people of all ages to come together. It is now an open place for encountering one's neigh-bours and participating in something together.

PROJECT
LE 56/ECO-INTERSTICE

ARCHITECT
**ATELIER D'ARCHITECTURE
AUTOGÉRÉE (AAA)**

LOCATION
PARIS, FRANCE

Multiple levels provide for multiple uses of the collective space

TESTIFY!
THE CONSEQUENCES OF ARCHITECTURE

LE 56/ECO-INTERSTICE
PARIS, FRANCE

**AN URBAN GARDEN BLOSSOMS IN PARIS'S SAINT-BLAISE
NEIGHBOURHOOD, BRINGING THE COMMUNITY TOGETHER IN
COOPERATION WITH PROFESSIONALS AND THE LOCAL GOVERNMENT.
CITY WALLS IN THE DENSE URBAN AREA BECOME AN OPPORTUNITY
FOR GROWTH AND A NEW ENVIRONMENTAL AWARENESS.**

CONTEXT

Atelier d'architecture autogérée (aaa), or the 'Studio for
Self-Managed Architecture', is a collective platform that
conducts explorations, actions and research concerning
urban mutations and emerging practices in the contemporary city. 'Urban tactics' are employed by aaa to
encourage the participation of inhabitants in the self-
management of disused urban spaces, to overpower
prejudices and stereotypes by proposing nomad and
reversible projects, and to initiate interstitial practices
that explore the potential of the city – in terms of
population, mobility and temporality. The area of the
city that this particular project took place in is very
dense, and the passageway in which the project was
completed was previously abandoned and considered
unalterable.

MISSION

It is through micro-political actions that the aaa collective
hopes to proactively participate in making the city more
ecological and more democratic, and to make urban
spaces less dependent on top-down processes and
more accessible to daily users. 'Self-managed architecture' is an architecture of relationships, processes
and personal agencies, as well as desires and skills.
Such architecture does not correspond to a liberal
practice but asks for new forms of association and
collaboration, based on exchange and reciprocity and
involving all those interested (individuals, organizations,
institutions), whatever the scale.

Inspiring projects from
around the world that
are currently bringing
nature back into our
cities range from urban
farming initiatives
to various guerrilla
gardening actions.
In many cases, they are
understood as direct
action against perceived
neglect or misuse of
abandoned space in the
city and assign a new
purpose to it.

The particular project 'Le 56/Eco-interstice' explores
the possibilities for an urban interstice to be transformed
into a collectively self-managed space. Initiated in 2006
in the Saint-Blaise area in the east of Paris, the project
engaged an unusual partnership between local governmental structures, local organizations, inhabitants of
the area and a professional association that runs training
programmes in eco-construction. The management of
the project gave space and time for construction, hoping
for the construction site itself to become a social and
cultural place of action.

REALIZATION

Initially occupied by mobile devices and temporary
installations, the plan evolved little by little into a
collectively managed space. The open building site
hosted different events, allowing participants to meet
each other and to participate in the decision-making
process during construction. The plot was designed
as an ecological interstice, hosting a greenhouse with
green roof and powered by solar panels. It includes
compost toilets, a rainwater collector, cultivation plots,
a compost laboratory, seed catchers and a wild bird
corridor. User participation takes on different scales
of proximity, relying on neighbourhood networks,
friendships and individual skills. The façade of the front
building is designed to unfold and open up, to create
a porous area at the ground floor level between the
plot and public space, allowing the collective garden to
invade the street. The structure allows for a multiplicity
of communal activities to coexist in both an indoor and
outdoor realm.

TESTIFY
THE CONSEQUENCES OF ARCHITECTURE

Parallel to the construction of the physical space, different social and cultural networks and relationships between the users and actors involved are continually emerging. The project has an important take on the notion of proximity and active borders. Neighbourhood walls transform the boundaries of the site into interactive devices, which – rather than separating – multiply possibilities for exchange and connection. Another strong aspect of the project is the ecological side; it focuses on energetic autonomy, recycling, leaving a minimal ecological footprint. Community members come together to create a sustainable environmental oasis in the midst of a dense urban setting.

COMMUNITY MEMBERS COME TOGETHER TO CREATE A SUSTAINABLE ENVIRONMENTAL OASIS IN THE MIDST OF A DENSE URBAN SETTING

◄ The Eco-Interstice occupies a long, narrow place between two buildings

▼ Residents gather to learn about gardening and meet each other

–
NAME
ANNE-MARIE VUYLSTEKE

NATIONALITY
FRENCH

OCCUPATION
PROFESSOR

LOCATION
PARIS, FRANCE
–

Please describe your neighbourhood in Paris, Saint-Blaise.
Three 100-m-high towers dominate the Saint-Blaise district – each is about 30 floors high and dates from the 1970s. Facing the community garden is the public garden Square des Cardeurs, which dates from the same period and is completely covered in concrete. This area is home to several social housing projects. The district is a self-enclosed residential area, and one of the most densely populated areas in Europe (800 inhabitants per square metre). About 40 years ago, the rue St-Blaise had many shops: five bakeries, several grocery shops, craftsmen, and so forth. It has a young population of people with nationalities who make modest incomes. Youth groups meet outside every day and in the summer things can get a bit heated at times. In general, though, the quality of life has been improving for the last five or six years. This area is pleasant to live in; there is little aggression here, and it's very quiet.

And the site where the garden is now? What was there before?
The garden is situated in an old alleyway that led to a factory that used to manufacture matches; this alley was then closed on both sides by gates, one side leading to the street and the other to the small courtyard belonging to a social housing project. Because of the lack of space, it has not been possible to build anything there. This place is wedged between two old Parisian buildings dating from the beginning of the twentieth century, and it's been used as a dump for a long time. People used to throw their clothespins, leftover food, glass, handkerchiefs, clothes, and so on out of their windows into the trash heap.

How did the garden begin? Did you have any input in the planning process? This project was initiated by the city council, with the

objective of revitalizing this place. I think the architecture firm was involved in this project at an early stage, because they suggested a participatory process involving the residents in an environmental and inexpensive process of transformation using cheap and ecological materials, aimed at promoting sustainable development. This project was in line with the city council's aspirations for ecological projects.

I took part in the first surveys: young people from AAA asked the local residents to answer some questions in order to find out what they wanted this place to be like in the future. It was funny; the young people were standing there, right in the middle of the street. I told them what I thought: I wanted this ugly place to become a green garden full of flowers!

How did it happen? What are the structures like? First, all the rubble and the litter had to be cleared away, and then tons of soil were brought in. Then, I remember that the house was built on piles and the installations were realized afterwards. A reintegration group called Apij worked for a long time, at least a year and a half, building the wooden shed, the storage places fitted with wooden pallets, the composting toilets and all the rest of the structures. The AAA architects were the main contractors. The height of the built-up elevation means that light floods the rooms in the structure. You get a good view of the street, and from the street, you can see shadows moving inside – it's all very nice! The idea was to avoid confining or restricting the space, to make it part of the street, to bring the outside inside. The building blends in very well with the neighbouring buildings, while being modern at the same time: I like this mix of wood, polycarbonate and bricks from the neighbouring buildings. It's quite an artistic achievement! The interesting thing is that it all fits in such a tiny,

'THIS PLACE IS WEDGED BETWEEN TWO OLD PARISIAN BUILDINGS DATING FROM THE BEGINNING OF THE TWENTIETH CENTURY, AND IT'S BEEN USED AS A DUMP FOR A LONG TIME'

reduced space: the autonomy of the place with the composting toilets, the compost, the solar panels for producing the place's own electricity, the tanks specially designed for collecting water and placed under the sloped roof of the shed, the green roof and the wood that creates such a warm atmosphere! I did not follow all the details of the process, but I know that the young people from the building site were very involved with the area during the time they worked there. I visited the building site from time to time to see how things were progressing, which was interesting. We were all, of course, invited to the official opening.

How have the neighbours responded to the project?

The premises are used as a community garden; about 30 individual parcels have been distributed among local residents who are members of the community garden and who are willing to become involved in various projects. The residents have really accepted this place. The neighbours nearby throw fewer things out of their windows and some of them come to the parties that are organized in the garden. Many neighbours respect this place; they turn down their music when seminars are taking place, which they didn't do at first. Apart from that, passers-by are very curious about the place, they enjoy dropping in when it's open and, once inside, they're enthusiastic. What is interesting is the process of reflection initiated by the architects, using the seminars that regularly take place in the garden: they are about ecology, environmental urban development projects, sustainable development, a non-conformist way of life, and so on. It's great for this area to benefit from this type of opening up to the world, to have the opportunity to attend fascinating seminars and events involving people from all over the world – and all that on your doorstep! This is a positive point for our district.

About a year ago, the architects encouraged us residents to organize ourselves and set up an association to run the place independently. It's true that they helped us along for quite some time and that they are still at hand if we need them. Slowly but surely, they also succeeded in making us realize what we ourselves can accomplish and helped us plan our own meetings and more culturally inspired projects. They showed us what collective participation and responsibility actually involves. They still organize seminars, attend the general meetings, support us with communication training (blogs) and give us advice.

Overall, has there been a positive change? Can you see an impact on a larger scale?
An AMAP association, promoting traditional agriculture, was set up here to sell farm produce once a week, which attracts quite a lot of residents. As far as I'm concerned, I think the district is more pleasant now than it used to be: it's great to have a place where you can do some gardening, see greenery in the middle of all those concrete blocks, meet friends easily, talk about cooking specialities, laugh and enjoy being outside, organize projects together, keep informed about ways of appropriating small places elsewhere in the city, and meet Parisian gardeners from other community gardens.

PROJECT
FAVELA PAINTING

CREATOR
**HAAS & HAHN /
JEROEN KOOLHAAS
AND DRE URHAHN**

LOCATION
RIO DE JANEIRO, BRAZIL

◀ Haas & Hahn lived in Rio for the duration of all of their projects

▲ Changing the *favela's* image can alter attitudes about the community

Page
cover /
229 /
233

FAVELA PAINTING
RIO DE JANEIRO, BRAZIL

**IN THE HEART OF RIO DE JANEIRO'S FAVELAS, THE DUTCH ARTIST DUO
HAAS & HAHN HAVE FOSTERED PRIDE AND CREATED JOBS BY PAINTING
ENORMOUS MURALS ON CONCRETE STRUCTURES AND RESIDENTIAL
FAÇADES. THROUGH COLOUR AND IMAGERY, THE NEIGHBOURHOODS
HAVE BEEN GIVEN A FRESH FACE AND A POINT OF MEDIA CONTACT
FROM WHICH TO PRESENT THEMSELVES ANEW.**

▲ View from the community out towards the ocean　　　　▶ Painting one of the countless vertical façades

CONTEXT

Rio de Janeiro's huge *favelas* are detrimental to the city's image, not only because of how they look, but because of what they represent. They are the embodiment of Rio's failure, the consequence of a city's inability to accommodate all of its citizens, physically and culturally. Over time, *favelas* like Vila Cruzeiro have gained reputations as immoral, terror-filled places. The impression isn't completely inaccurate, but it exacts a price on *favela* residents, most of whom are not involved in the drug-related violence that fills the nightly news.

Another famous example of chromatic interventions in urban space is the painting of grey communist buildings in bright colours (bright yellow, green and violet) in Albania's capital Tirana, ordered by the city's socialist mayor and former artist Edi Rama, who was named World Mayor in 2004.

MISSION

In 2006, the Dutch artist duo Haas & Hahn started developing the idea of creating community-driven art interventions in Brazil. Their efforts yielded two murals that were painted in Vila Cruzeiro, Rio's most notorious slum, in collaboration with local youths. The project's ambition is to create imagery to counter the steady stream of negative coverage of Rio's *favelas*.

'If you want to build a bridge between these two sides of the city that live side by side but have an enormous gap between them,' Urhahn has said, 'the easiest way is to do it through some sort of art intervention.' Koolhaas added: 'We tried to find a way for the [residents'] sense of pride to be painted on the walls of the *favela* so that the outside world could see how good they feel about themselves and could understand that there are families here that can take care of themselves.'

TESTIFY!
THE CONSEQUENCES OF ARCHITECTURE

◄ This painting was based on a tattoo design   ▲ The project provides jobs for residents

REALIZATION

The first painting, finished in 2007, was a 150-m² mural depicting a boy flying a kite, which is a popular pastime in the *favelas*. The painting took three months to finish and was made together with local youths, who were found through the Soldados Nunca Mais programme of the Ibiss foundation. The second large painting in Vila Cruzeiro was finished in 2008. It was situated on a massive concrete structure that was originally built to protect the hill from mudslides during the rainy season. It was painted together with local youths, who learned a craft and earned wages from their work. Urhahn says: 'There is a social and political statement in saying "in this slum where there are so many difficulties and so much bad press, let's make something that is totally detached from that, something that's just beautiful".' After eight months of painting, enduring long periods of rain, shootings and police occupation, the 2000-m² work of art was finally finished.

Even though the project doesn't fix any of the major problems the favelas are facing, Favela Painting is much more than just a simple cosmetic change of the urban realm.

The Favela Painting project attracted intense media interest in Brazil and abroad. The more recent painting, Rio Cruzeiro, was covered by news agencies around the world, and in Brazil the project attracted reporters from every major newspaper and TV station. For GLOBO TV in Brazil, the visit to the unveiling of Haas & Hahn's second mural was the first time it had sent a crew to Vila Cruzeiro since one of its reporters was murdered there while investigating drug dealing. For the artists, this positive coverage meant a chance to bridge the gap between the neighbourhood's perception and its reality. Over their months of work there, Haas & Hahn have built up trusting relationships with people in a community that has grown weary of outsiders. 'It's an interesting situation when you're an employer, but you have to ask your employees how to walk the streets,' Urhahn says. 'Everything that doesn't have to do with paint, they know better. And for that they're really invaluable to the project.'

–
NAME
**DRE URHAHN,
JEROEN KOOLHAAS**

NATIONALITY
DUTCH

OCCUPATION
ARTIST

LOCATION
**AMSTERDAM/ROTTERDAM,
THE NETHERLANDS**
–

How did you end up in the community? What were your first encounters with the place?
We were introduced to this particular community (Vila Cruzeiro) by Nanko van Buuren, a Dutchman who runs several social projects all around Rio. We were looking for a place to 'test run' our project idea and this notorious slum seemed most in need of something positive. In the beginning people were wary of us, as the idea of making art in a war zone seemed strange to them. For us it was hard as well, to learn how the inhabitants of this community tried to live 'normal' lives in such a surreal environment.

What were your expectations for the place before you got there? How did reality differ from expectations? Having made a documentary about youth in Brazilian slums, we were already aware of the warm social cohesion within these communities. But this particular place was armed so heavily by the local drug gang, that it seemed impossible to somehow fit in. Our project made it very easy though. Working with the local kids and spending all our time within, we soon found ourselves embraced by the community. Very soon I even moved into a house in Vila Cruzeiro and felt more at home than I had felt on the 'outside'.

How did the project evolve over time? How did it come to fruition? Our project grew, not only in size, but also in methodology. As it was born out of a playful idea ('What if we could paint a whole *favela*?') we started with no more than a sketch, a bunch of paint and two kids. Over time we learned how to professionalize our production and our designs, so we would be able to create more result in less time. When the media picked it up and started to spread the news about our work worldwide, we realized we were on to something special.

What were the most memorable or unexpected events? There are almost too many things to tell. Some heart-warming, others heartbreaking. I will never forget an old lady coming up to us, telling us that she had prayed all her life for God to send her a sign, but never had expected that to be two Dutch painters, turning her street into a marvel. But by far the most valuable effect personally are all the wonderful friendships I've made over time, which have had an incredible impact on me as a person.

What long-term effects did you expect? What happened after each phase, and what is the situation now? One of our goals was to open up the conversation about slums in Brazil. Getting Vila Cruzeiro on the cover of every newspaper with a positive message changed the perception of the public. On a personal level, we saw how serious our painters took the chance they were offered. For them to get an alternative to a life of crime that they could be proud of came at an important moment in their life. Years later, they still talk about the investment we made in them and what effect it has had on them. Hopefully they themselves will act as an example for other kids.

Can you think of a way to improve upon the project? What are your hopes for its future? In our eyes this project has a lot more potential. By adding more educational elements and teaching locals to continue the project themselves, the possibilities could be almost endless. The main problem is financing. With more money, we could set up more projects and take the idea to other cities, countries or even continents.

–
NAME
NANKO G. VAN BUUREN

NATIONALITY
DUTCH/BRAZILIAN

OCCUPATION
**DIRECTOR OF IBISS,
BRAZILIAN INNOVATION INSTITUTE
ON SOCIAL HEALTH AND DIRECTOR
OF IBISS PRODUÇÕES CULTURAIS,
PRESIDENT OF UNITED CULTURES
FOR DEVELOPMENT**

LOCATION
RIO DE JANEIRO, BRAZIL
–

–
'THIS *FAVELA* NOW BELONGS TO THE SO-CALLED "PACIFIED" AREAS OF RIO DE JANEIRO'
–

You are familiar with the site of Haas & Hahn's Favela Painting project? Yes. One of the projects by Jeroen Koolhaas and Dre Urhahn is situated in the socially excluded and extreme violent *favela* Vila Cruzeiro in the neighbourhood of Penha. The *favela* is built on the hillsides of Complexo da Penha. The main problem the community is facing is the drug trade, which provokes heavy confrontations with the police, with a lot of victims on both sides – among the so-called *soldados* of the drug trade as well as the slum inhabitants through stray bullets. Sanitation is very poor in Vila Cruzeiro and there is often a lack of water. The community suffers the risk of landslides during heavy rainfall.

What was the state of the site before the project began and how did the project arise? Five years ago a part of Vila Cruzeiro suffered a landslide. A part of the hillside came down, together with around 120 houses. With the help of the State of Rio de Janeiro, IBISS and the Community Council of Vila Cruzeiro made a con-crete construction on the land-slide area to avoid new landslides. Stairs were made in this ugly grey concrete construction to facilitate the inhabitants on the top of the hill. Some years ago Haas & Hahn had already developed the idea to make big paintings in the *favelas* on the walls of existing houses. Their first experiment took place in Vila Cruzeiro, where they painted a boy with a kite on three houses behind the central soccer field of Espaço IBISS. Based on the positive reactions of the slum inhabitants, Haas & Hahn developed the idea to make more and bigger paintings in the *favelas*. The enormous concrete construction on the former landslide site offered an interesting space for them to realize a bigger project. Haas & Hahn discussed it with the Community Council, which proved very interested in it. Together with a

tattoo artist they started to elaborate an artistic design for the stairs and surrounding area: a Japanese waterfall with golden carp. They showed the inhabitants of Vila Cruzeiro the design and it was immediately accepted.

What was the implementation process like after the approval of the original design by the community? Jeroen and Dre drew the outlines of the design on the concrete, adapting it in some areas to the surface and construction. After the rough design was laid out, they contracted three youngsters from Vila Cruzeiro to help them colour the large-scale piece. It took them more than half a year of hard daily labour to finish the work, during which time Haas & Hahn lived right in the local community. After the project was finished the artists revisited the community twice and they're still in touch with the youngsters who helped them realize the work.

Was the project well-received by the community members and what is the site like now? Yes, the inhabitants of Vila Cruzeiro very much like it. It makes them proud to have a work of art in the *favela* that attracts so much media attention all over the world. This *favela* now belongs to the so-called 'pacified' areas of Rio de Janeiro, where the drug gangs have been kicked out through a dominant military presence. Therefore many people visit the site to see the painting, and the local bars make some extra money by selling water and beer to the visitors. But even though the community members really try to minimize the wear-off of the paint, the art work is changing little by little and will eventually disappear because of natural conditions such as heavy rain and sunshine.

PROJECT
SKATEISTAN

CREATOR
**SKATEISTAN /
ACCL, ANOC,
OLIVER PERCOVICH**

LOCATION
KABUL, AFGHANISTAN

TESTIFY!
THE CONSEQUENCES OF ARCHITECTURE

Skateistan runs several educational programmes besides skate classes

SKATEISTAN
KABUL, AFGHANISTAN

**AFGHANISTAN'S – AND THE WORLD'S – FIRST SKATEBOARDING
SCHOOL EMPOWERS KABUL'S YOUTH TO TAKE THEIR FUTURES
INTO THEIR OWN HANDS, GIVING AFGHANI CHILDREN A RARE
OPPORTUNITY TO LEARN AND HAVE FUN, AND IN THE PROCESS
TEACHING SO MUCH MORE THAN A SPORT.**

In Afghanistan, sport is seen as a male activity

CONTEXT

With 68 per cent of the population under the age of 25 (and 50 per cent under the age of 16), it is vital that development efforts in Afghanistan engage with the youth immediately; only then will Afghanistan's youngest citizens be able to claim ownership of the problems they will soon inherit. For this to happen, children need safe and supportive environments to interact non-violently, gain self-confidence and learn important skills. Safe activities for children in most of Afghanistan are extremely limited, especially for girls. Sports are a constructive way for children to interact, but many popular Afghan sports — football, volleyball, buzkashi, kite flying and even bike riding — are seen as male activities, and females are almost always excluded from participating in them.

MISSION

In 2007, Oliver Percovich and Sharna Nolan arrived in Kabul with little more than a couple of skateboards. Ollie and Sharna soon discovered that their boards drew in local children like an unstoppable magnetic force. They began regular skateboarding sessions in an abandoned Russian fountain in the district of Mekroyan,

The urban practice of skateboarding offers a completely alternative view, or use, of the city that tests the boundaries of the urban environment by threatening conventional definitions of space. Skaters radically subvert the intended use of the city and its buildings by using its structural elements in a way neither practiced nor understood by most 'normal' civilians.

and a group of local boys began to join them. Then came the girls. Thankfully, Afghans largely consider skateboarding a suitable activity for girls. These initial sessions, informal at first, eventually led to the foundation of Skateistan, Afghanistan's (and the world's) first co-educational skateboard school.

Operating as an independent, neutral, Afghan NGO, the school engages growing numbers of urban and internally-displaced youths in Afghanistan through skateboarding, and provides them with new opportunities in cross-cultural interaction, education and personal empowerment. Skateistan's students come from all of Afghanistan's diverse ethnic and socio-economic backgrounds. They not only develop skills in skateboarding, but also healthy habits, civic responsibility, information technology, the arts and foreign language skills. The students themselves decide what they want to learn — Skateistan connects them with teachers who will enable them to develop the skills that they consider important. Skateistan provides a safe and supportive environment where trust is built not only between participants, but that reaches across the Afghan-Western divide.

The NGO is also developing the students' abilities to express their opinions on the issues that concern them, enabling them to fulfil their visions for the future of their country. It empowers students to find solutions to the problems they face through social asset-building activities and youth development forums; it also broadcasts their voices (with the consent of their parents and communities) over the radio, in documentaries and in print media.

Skateboarding is a non-competitive global sport that requires minimal supervision and resources. Achievements in skateboarding are individual and depend on balance, creativity and personal expression. Skating can be practiced anywhere there is a smooth surface; it brings young people together to be active and communicative. Considering the country's recent political history — not to mention its longstanding social barriers — Skateistan believes that the community-building effects of skateboarding will be especially visible in Afghanistan.

REALIZATION

On 29 October 2009, Skateistan completed construction of an all-inclusive skate park and educational facility on 5,428 m2 of land donated by the Afghan National Olympic Committee. At the Skateistan facility, over 300 regular students receive training from experienced skateboarders in a secure environment. Skateboards, shoes and safety equipment are loaned on-site for the duration of classes. Currently, there are 18 classroom sessions being held per week. In addition to teaching girls' journalism classes, advanced art classes, a theatre programme and classes about environmental health, Skateistan runs a Back-to-School programme that helps children enrol or re-enrol in public school. Skateistan also works with physically and mentally challenged Afghans. The NGO has developed a specialized curriculum for disabled youths that uses skateboarding to provide mobility and sports therapy. Skateistan strives to tell a positive story about Afghan youth, using global media platforms to send a message of hope, unity and peace. A documentary, Skateistan – The Movie , will soon be released, detailing the construction of the school, the achievements of its students, and what it's like to grow up in twenty-first-century Afghanistan.

◀ 68 per cent of Afghanistan's population is under 25 years old

▼ Inside Skateistan's indoor skate park

NAME
MAX HENNINGER

NATIONALITY
GERMAN

OCCUPATION
DEPUTY DIRECTOR OF SKATEISTAN

LOCATION
KABUL, AFGHANISTAN
–

What is life like in Kabul? Of the population, 68 per cent is under 25, and 50 per cent is under the age of 16. With so many young people and a serious lack of infrastructure, recreational activities for young people in the city are largely limited to soccer and kite flying in the busy city streets. Also, these activities are considered inappropriate for girls.

How is Skateistan about more than just skateboarding? After spending a considerable amount of time skateboarding with children in the streets of Kabul, as well as at an old fountain left by the Russians in a neighbourhood called Macroyan, it became apparent that both boys and girls could benefit from a more stable sporting environment. Watching young people interact with one another on skateboards also led to the idea that education could become a part of participating in sports.

What happens at the Skateistan facility in Kabul? Where is it and who built it? Skateistan's indoor facility was built on the Afghan National Olympic Grounds next to Ghazi Stadium. The building was constructed from the ground up by a local company called ACCL. In addition to the indoor skate park facility, two classrooms, two changing rooms with showers and lockers, an office and conference area, a multi-sport area, and a climbing wall have been built. Having a 1750-m^2 facility has allowed for all sorts of programming to develop in a more stable and consistent environment.

What individuals, agencies, aid organizations, companies or community groups were involved in the design process? First there was Oliver Percovich, Skateistan's executive director, who recognizes that the safety of all staff, volunteers and participants is a top priority. There was

–

'WATCHING YOUNG PEOPLE INTERACT WITH ONE ANOTHER ON SKATEBOARDS ALSO LED TO THE IDEA THAT EDUCATION COULD BECOME A PART OF PARTICIPATING IN SPORTS'

–

also a contribution by General Zahir Aghbar, who is obviously concerned about Skateistan's safety as it affects the larger Olympic grounds as well. Other design input came from engineer Moheen at ACCL construction company, who did not give input on security matters but rather on the design itself.

Are you still in touch with the architects? Are there any further projects planned? Yes, we are in touch with the architects, since we are planning to build another facility in Masar-e Sharif in northern Afghanistan. At the Kabul facility, modifications have been made in- and outside of the facility. We recently finalized a proper guttering of the roof as well as a ventilation system. Inside the park we have just built a climbing wall and a multisport floor for which only local materials were used.

How fast did things happen at the facility in Kabul? Has it been a success? What is happening there now? The facility was built within three months. The design didn't change during the building process. ACCL, the Afghan construction company that built the facility, mainly used materials available in local markets. Also, local labourers were employed throughout the whole building process. The structure has been used for all sorts of things since it opened on 29 October 2009. There is regular weekly programming that includes one hour of skateboarding and one hour of classroom time for Skateistan students, as well as specialized classes for disabled boys, art, and journalism, among other things. The facility has also been used for a variety of special events: Go Skateboarding Day, new semester celebrations, art exhibitions, and Peace Day events, to name a few.

Do people in the community like the facility? What do they think of Skateistan? As far as I know there

has been significant local support for the project from the start, especially on the part of General Zahir Aghbar, President of the Afghanistan National Olympic Committee (ANOC). He gave Skateistan a piece of land to build the facility on within the Olympic grounds and a ten-year lease. The facility and the programming of Skateistan are quite well received by the community. There are always hundreds of people that attend special events, and there is always good feedback from both international and local media, as well as from students' families. The project has had a really positive overall effect on the community. There have been many times when students have told us, especially the girls, that the first day they came to Skateistan was the best day of their lives. Having the facility has created an environment where so many things are possible, but most importantly it has created a space for kids to be themselves. Skateistan facilitates not only sport, but the opportunity for young people to build relationships with one another and with Skateistan staff and volunteers, as well as to take on leadership roles in their community.

What challenges does Skateistan face? How have these problems been taken into account? Many, many places in Afghanistan have to consider that they may become a target of violence, especially places that are known to have foreigners working inside. Being on the Olympic grounds is actually quite good because we have more protection than we likely would have otherwise. There are fences around the grounds and gates staffed by ANOC's guards. We are also surrounded by Afghan organizations and operate as an Afghan NGO ourselves, so I think the risks of violence are small compared to other organizations working here. That said, it is of course a concern, for both the safety of the staff and the children coming here six

days a week. One of the main facility designers was Skateistan's executive director, Oliver Percovich, who is very conscious of any way that the organization can minimize risk. I think more of a concern when designing a sports complex in Afghanistan is figuring out how to ensure the privacy of the girls that are coming to skate here. At present we have small windows, and fences keep people at a distance. Soon, with the help of Convic Design in Australia, we will have an outdoor skate park/recreation area with trees and high fences creating a secure, private area for our students, particularly the females. Being inconspicuous and blending in with the rest of the Olympic facilities is important from an aesthetic perspective, and also a security concern on some level. At the same time, Skateistan's facility needs to be functional above all else, which is why the K-Span design seemed ideal because within this simple basic structure there are many possibilities for interior design. I think the bright Afghan colours help show that this is a place where children come to have fun.

Does the project still rely on international aid to run? The project is still moving towards being self-sustainable. There are several projects in the works to make this happen. Skateistan is being developed into a social brand, which means that there is a variety of Skateistan merchandise and co-branded products that directly support the project in Kabul. We're also working on increasing private funding through private donations and fundraisers from Skateistan's international entities. Any of the money donated to Skateistan is used to run classes, pay staff and maintain or improve the facility.

REACH OUT

—

SPACES FOR LEARNING AND COMMUNITY

3

PROJECT
BRIDGE SCHOOL

ARCHITECT
LI XIAODONG ATELIER

LOCATION
XIASHI VILLAGE, CHINA

TESTIFY!
THE CONSEQUENCES OF ARCHITECTURE

The Bridge School spans a creek that runs through the village

Page
228 / 233

BRIDGE SCHOOL
XIASHI VILLAGE, CHINA

**A BRIDGE CONNECTING TWO ANCIENT FORTRESSES IN A RURAL CHINESE
VILLAGE HOUSES A SCHOOL AND REJUVENATES THE LOCAL ECONOMY,
WHILE CAREFULLY CONSIDERING THE LINK BETWEEN PAST AND FUTURE
ARCHITECTURE AND HARMONIZING WITH ITS ENVIRONMENT.**

View of traditional rammed earth building and entrance situation of Bridge School

CONTEXT

China's rapid modernization has caused stark contrasts between old and new structures, opening a rupture between past and present architectures, and leaving many rural areas undeveloped and unconnected to the rapidly changing appearance of urban areas. Rural Fujian province, on China's south-east coast, is a mountainous region with a humid, subtropical climate – it has traditionally been described as 'eight parts mountain, one part water, and one part farmland'. The small village of Xiashi in Fujian has few new buildings. For several years Xiashi had been in need of not only a primary school, but a new community centre to provide a central, social space.

Rammed earth is an ancient building method using the raw materials of earth, chalk, lime and gravel that has seen a revival in recent years as people seek more sustainable building materials and natural building methods.

MISSION

The main goal of the Bridge School's design was to rejuvenate Xiashi's community and to sustain the traditional culture and lifestyle through a contemporary aesthetic language that does not compete with tradition, but instead presents and communicates with tradition in new ways. When architect Li Xiaodong was asked to design the school, he had the inspiration to place it on a bridge between the two ancient *toulou* – traditional fortress-like structures – on either side of the river that runs through the village. Originally constructed by ancestors of the local Hakka people, these distinctive circular fortresses have thick, sturdy walls of rammed earth. The structure that bridges the two halves of the village is intended to symbolically connect the past to the future.

The bridge unites two ancient round fortresses called *toulous*

THE CONCEPT FOR THE BUILDING WAS INSPIRED BY TRADITIONAL CHINESE MEDICINE

—

REALIZATION

Supported by concrete piers, the simple steel structure acts like a giant box girder that's been slightly dislocated, so the building subtly twists, rises and falls as it spans the creek. Inside is a pair of almost identical, wedge-shaped classrooms, each tapering towards the mid-point of the structure. Although it's possible to use the main building as a bridge, a narrow crossing suspended underneath the steel structure and anchored by tensile wires offers an alternative and more direct route.

Following this holistic approach the various functions of the body or building are carefully balanced. The building-body is seen in terms of a system of organs, based loosely on particular functions, rather than in terms of its isolated parts or organs.

Included in the building plan is a playground for the children on one side of the water. Physical lightness and spatial fluidity are key elements of the structure. By means of sliding and folding doors, the school can be transformed into an impromptu theatre or play structure. This ability for movement appeals to children and encourages them to actively engage with the architecture. The steel frame is wrapped in a veil of slim timber slats, which filter light and temper the interior with cooling breezes. The lightweight and airy structure appears in stark contrast to the heavy stone architecture on either side of the creek.

The concept for the building was inspired by traditional Chinese medicine, which sees the human being as a complete system with interconnected parts. Approaching the project this way allowed for consideration of the community as a whole to create a flexible and graceful building. The Bridge School achieves unity at many levels: between past and present, between traditional and modern, between the two riverbanks, and between members of the community. The construction has successfully enlivened the community, addressing social needs through architectural intervention.

▲ Movable screens allow for many spatial configurations

▼ The school is a social space

NAME
CHEN JIANSHENG

NATIONALITY
CHINESE

OCCUPATION
ARCHITECT

LOCATION
BEIJING, CHINA

How well do you know Xiashi Village? Can you describe the village? I'm originally from the county that Xiashi Village lies in. According to the census, there are about a thousand people living in the Xiashi community. Half of the population seeks job opportunities in urban areas outside the village, and most of those that stay in the community are farmers or run small businesses. Most of the village's old buildings were abandoned. Compared to other villages, this is a rather poverty-stricken one; half of the farmers do not have enough food to feed themselves and their families.

How did you link Li Xiaodong with the project? I was a member of Li Xiaodong Atelier, and I spent a lot of time in that studio even when I was still in college. On one occasion, Li Xiaodong was talking about the 'Hope Primary Schools' project, and I told him the situation of my rural hometown. I have always been interested in the *tulous* (ancient circular fortress-like buildings), so I also told him about their situation. Historical *tulous* are aplenty in our county, but the number is decreasing drastically and the local authorities are unable to do anything to preserve them – they don't have the expertise to do so. It seemed like we should design something for the *tulous*. In Xiashi only two remained. These were on the verge of falling down. The place looked abandoned when we visited for the first time in 2008 – it was overgrown with weeds. It used to be the centre of the village, but had become a wilderness, a wasteland. After some research, it came to our knowledge that the villagers had left the buildings about 20 years ago. All that remained were two tiny pathways.

So you and Li Xiaodong were the primary project planners? I kept contact with the locals throughout the process, and Li Xiaodong and I orchestrated the project and were its chief designers. The project started over the summer, in July, and we recruited some student helpers who had just graduated. Li and I were in charge of the design, and the students helped out. Once the plan was finalized, I went back to my hometown in Fujian and looked for construction workers to do the preparatory work. Until I returned to my hometown, I didn't realize that there were a lot of issues we hadn't considered.

Like what? What challenges did you face in the process? We spent two months working on the structural design and drawing the floor plan, and then meetings between workers and designers were arranged. At the very beginning, the designers didn't show much interest in the project – they were more concerned about its commercial value. We found it difficult to work for them, since for us it was purely about charity. It took a while for them to understand what we really wanted and finally they were able to help. The next problem we had was with the team of workers. Originally, we intended to let one team of workers finish the whole project, but we soon found that the project was not as easy as we had thought, and most of the workers didn't have the necessary skills. This project was very technical and there were a lot of details and nuances that needed to be taken care of. I sent an email to Li and told him all the problems, and then I decided to take care of the project organization myself. I started looking for funding, materials, workers, and so forth. It took almost a year for me to get things done.

A lot of people helped us. Once the design institute really delved into the project, they offered us support in the structural design. This is the unique part of the project. The designers from the institute made some changes in the structure, and some good effects were generated from their design. During the process we met a lot of workers. Some were bricklayers, some were carpenters. We had a lot of discussions with them and they certainly had a strong influence on us.

Did you change the design to accommodate these challenges and various inputs of opinion? Yes – there were a lot of complexities in the site. We underestimated the diversity of the building site. At the beginning we hired a team of local surveyors, but most of the information we got from them was not accurate. After the weeding was done, the site brought us a lot of surprises. We made changes to our design accordingly, and it is what you see now.

The most obvious change is that the location of the site is different – we were planning to use villagers' land. However, the villagers were unwilling to let us use the land, and they refused to accept any compensation for it. It took a while to get the matter settled. Another major change is the bridge. The radian and the length of the bridge were not the same as what you see now. A dragon-eye tree would have had to be cut down for the original plan, but we wanted to keep the tree, so we made changes to the bridge. Now the bridge looks wider and more stretchy. It's also a little bit longer than before, and it looks much better.

The most notable part of this architecture is its evolution through a problem-solving process. What we considered at the beginning was very different from what we went through during the process. We underestimated the challenges this building brought to us. The input from the local villagers was important. Whenever I encountered problems I talked to them, and gradually we would come up with a solution. We were lucky that we were able to find the people we needed, and ended up spending less money to complete the project.

What materials and labour did you end up using? All the materials are local except for the structural steel. Regarding the labourers, except those installing the structural steel, all were local. The wood, the stones, the sand, the cobblestones, and the plants – all are local materials.

The bridge has a steel structure. Before setting up the structure, we needed to work on the foundation. Originally the institute came up with a modern design for the bridge piers, but we couldn't find local people with the necessary skills to build them, and we had a limited budget. Foundation piling was required for that design, which would be very expensive. We spent some time to look for piling workers but we discovered that we didn't have the budget and they didn't possess the skills. Considering all the limitations, we decided to go for a 'con-

joined foundation' – that is, one that connects the two piles on each side of the foundation. Then we dug the foundation to let the piles join together and strengthen each other. They are just as solid as those bridge piers for the flyovers. So, in the end, we didn't follow the design provided by the institute. The changes we made saved resources and money, and matched our requirements. The ground was very solid. And actually, after digging up the foundation we discovered there were stones underneath. This further consolidated the foundation.

The width of the steel structure is more than 20 m. This was the biggest challenge to us. It cost us to put a crane on the site. We negotiated with the local authorities and agreed to build a path for the villagers. In return we were allowed to put the crane on the site. You may not be able to see that path now, because we have restored it to the original landscape. We talked to a villager and asked him to tear down his house. We compensated him and also rebuilt the house for him.

How did the villagers react? They have changed their attitudes a lot since the beginning, which we found to be really interesting. At first, the local villagers had no idea what we wanted to do. There were a lot of difficulties. But when the construction was completed, people realized that the building not only made a change to the landscape, but also brought visitors to the village. Sometimes activities were held there, too. The building has brought advantages to both villagers and visitors. It has brought them more business, and enhanced their environment. Villagers now have a more positive attitude towards the architecture than they did at the start. I can tell how their feelings have changed compared to the first time I talked to them.

And now? Who is running the bridge school? Because I was working on-site, I was able to talk to the local authorities. The building eventually has to be managed by the local authorities, so it will be run by the authorities and the villagers. I started collaboration with them from the very beginning. If they needed me, or when I had the need to talk to them, we would just work together. There is a manager overseeing everything at the moment.

There have been no alterations to the building itself, but there are regular maintenance checks. Because of our limited budget, there are places that needed to be worked on. But we have done some maintenance in those places, and the issues are now very minor.

Does the community embrace the new building now? To me, the most meaningful part of this project is how the building itself has altered the area's landscape. In this case, the values of the *tulous* are recognized. The building itself is just a piece of hardware, an addition to the original structures. It has changed how people think. In the past, they were indifferent to the *tulous* and to our ideas about them, but once the project was completed they saw the values of the ancient architecture. A lot of visitors come to this area now, not just because of the bridge school, but also because of the two *tulous*. They want to see the environment and how people live here. This bridge is what made people change their attitudes.

PROJECT
**MARIA GRAZIA CUTULI
PRIMARY SCHOOL**

ARCHITECT
**2A+P, IAN+ AND MA0 /
EMMEAZERO WITH
MARIO CUTULI**

LOCATION
HERAT, AFGHANISTAN

▲ A wall surrounding the school provides protection

▼ Students gather together for roll call

MARIA GRAZIA CUTULI PRIMARY SCHOOL
HERAT, AFGHANISTAN

INSIDE THESE COLOURFUL SCHOOL BUILDINGS SURROUNDED BY GARDENS AND FRUIT TREES, TEACHERS WILL BEGIN TO COMBAT AFGHANISTAN'S STAGGERING RATES OF ILLITERACY. THE PROJECT WAS INSPIRED BY MARIA GRAZIA CUTULI, AN ITALIAN JOURNALIST WHO WAS KILLED IN 2001 IN AFGHANISTAN, AND WAS SUPPORTED BY THE FOUNDATION NAMED AFTER HER WITH THE UNDERSTANDING THAT THE LACK OF KNOWLEDGE BEGETS VIOLENCE.

CONTEXT

In 2001, Maria Grazia Cutuli, a prominent Italian correspondent for the Milan-based daily *Corriere della Sera*, was murdered by a group of gunmen who ambushed her convoy in Afghanistan. After this tragic event, her family established the Maria Grazia Cutuli Foundation that aims to support social and educational programmes for women and children in countries devastated by war or natural calamities, focusing on Afghanistan. The foundation provided all necessary funds for the construction of the Maria Grazia School in western Afghanistan's Herat Province. The Herat area has a heavy military presence and very little public infrastructure. Women in particular are at a disadvantage when it comes to education in Afghanistan. Recent estimates report that 57 per cent of men and 87 per cent of women in Afghanistan are illiterate.

The site of the school is a dry, dusty, flat piece of land in Kush Rod village, bordered on the north by the dark Hindu Kush Mountains. The beauty of Afghanistan's natural landscape, described in Maria Grazia Cutuli's articles, gave the architects initial ideas and inspiration for the school's design.

The Italian journalist was shot at the age of 30 on the road to Kabul, together with a group of international correspondents. A number of documentaries have been made about her life. Among the most recent are *Il Prezzo de la Verità* (The Price of Truth), which tries to reconstruct the private and professional life of Cutuli via dozens of interviews, and *È lì che bisogna essere. Per testimoniare* (That's where you have to be. To testify).

MISSION

The school was designed to provide an environment conducive to innovative teaching, as opposed to typical emergency reconstruction models built according to immediate need without functional considerations. The workgroup wanted to use local materials and technologies, and figure out a way to use outdoor areas as 'green classrooms', lessening the environmental impact. The school's library was designed to act as an important meeting space for the community and stand as a landmark for the whole village. After several meetings supported by sketches and study models, the workgroup chose an articulated layout: a series of linked boxes housing the classrooms and corridors. The only two-storey structure is the library. Border walls, necessary for security reasons, define and enclose the space.

REALIZATION

After the first stone setting, building started immediately and proceeded very quickly. All the materials and the applied technologies have been defined according to local uses. Afghan workers carefully followed the drawings made by the architects, but according to their own construction processes. For instance, while the architects would have built the structural frame before the walls, Afghani workers constructed all the elements – foundation, pillars, walls – at once, adding beams and a roof at the very end. Every week the architecture office received reports, pictures and updates from the local project director, and at the end of November 2010, three members of the workgroup visited the site to determine how to finish the structure.

The structure of the building is a reinforced concrete frame enclosed by solid bricks. Between the eight enclosed classrooms there are small and intimate outdoor

◀ The school's includes eight classroom units   ▲ Gardens will teach about agriculture   ▼ Opening day was a happy occasion

▲ The painted façades reference colours often used in Afghanistan

▶ Girls have equal learning opportunities at Maria Grazia School

THERE ARE SMALL AND INTIMATE OUTDOOR SPACES WHERE CHILDREN CAN PLAY AND RELAX UNDER THE SHADE OF ABOUT 50 FRUIT TREES

spaces where children can play and relax under the shade of about 50 fruit trees. Several varied vegetable gardens serve as a natural extension of the classrooms. The main courtyard at the centre of the group of buildings provides a central outdoor gathering place.

The orientation of the classrooms assures the right amount of daylight and natural ventilation. Every façade and border wall will be painted different shades of blue, a colour commonly used in Afghanistan, and the iron-framed windows will be painted red. The colours of the structure will help make it a recognizable landmark that is visible from a distance. The *Corriere della Sera* will donate 50 computers to the school, and the Provincial Administration of Catania, Italy will fund the realization of a school playground. The school opened in April 2011.

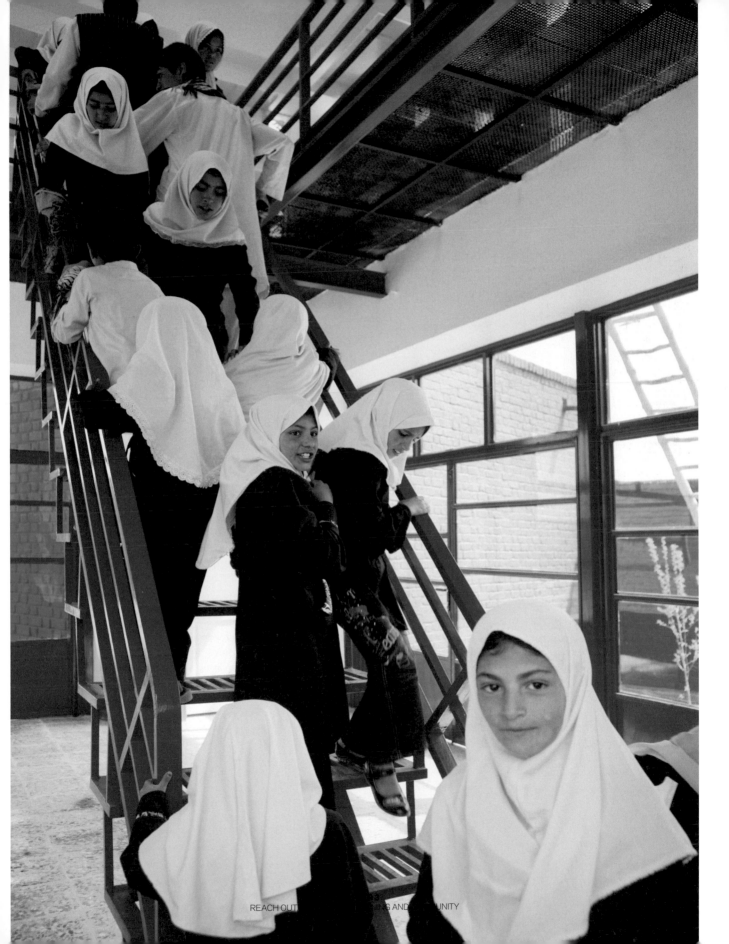

—
NAME
ANTONIO OTTOMANELLI

NATIONALITY
ITALIAN

OCCUPATION
PHOTOGRAPHER

LOCATION
MILAN, ITALY
—

—
'THE ARCHITECTURE OF THE EXTERIOR AND THE INTERIOR APPEARED HUMBLE AND COURAGEOUS AT THE SAME TIME. IT COMBINES A SOMEWHAT HAND-MADE POP ARCHITECTURAL STANCE WITH THE POETRY OF A MONUMENTAL CRAFT'
—

You have spent considerable time in Afghanistan as a photographer?
Yes, I first left for Afghanistan in order to start a photographic research project in the Middle East investigating the relationship between identity and crisis as an index of development. I'm planning to continue this research on issues related to architectural reconstruction and infrastructure in a country in a state of emergency. Having spent some time in these regions, I realized that it is impossible to understand or translate in pictures or words the complexity of the Middle East and Islam in general and Afghanistan in particular, or what is officially called a 'peace mission' but is in fact nothing but a war. On my travels through Afghanistan I am constantly reminded of a paragraph by Nathaniel Hawthorne quoted by Paul Auster at the beginning of his novel In the Country of Last Things: 'Not long ago, passing through the dreams gate, I visited that region of the Earth in which is the famous City of Destruction.'

How did your first contact with the school project in Herat arise?
I've been to Herat a couple of times. It's very different than the rest of the country. It was founded by Alexander the Great and served as cultural centre of higher learning under the Persians. Today, Herat's paediatric hospital is one of the most important projects realized with Italian support in this region. It is actually the second-largest hospital of its kind in Afghanistan, with a catchment area of about a million people. Yet the Herat hospital has a high rate of mortality: five children die every day – not from specific or chronic pathologies, but just because there isn't enough medicine. Children simply die waiting for medicine. But that's another of Afghanistan's sad daily truths. So, when I arrived at the construction site of the school with my driver Ahmet and his prophetically bearded, ex-mujaheddin uncle, the work on site was in full progress. You have to understand that there are no names for streets in most of Afghanistan. Urbanism is rather liquid

here, you navigate by sight. However, as soon as we arrived we were kindly welcomed by the master builder and the project manager outside the low red brick wall fencing off the site from the surrounding area. Being in this remote location in desperate need of so many basic things of life, I realized how important a tool architecture can be. A building, especially one dedicated to education, really means something. Here architecture is useful.

Can you elaborate on your impression of the building site?
The building site seemed very organized. I've seen worse places in Italy, in surely more expensive yards. At the time that saw the school, the project was nearly finished. Only the windows and blue plaster were missing. Back then the building merged with the colours of the earth and seemed no different from the typical rural village architecture of the region. The typical fence-like enclosure of the building reflects the somewhat tribal nature of Afghan society, in which

each family is a tribe defined by its very own boundaries. The thick and compact building structure made from local red bricks also provides the best seasonal temperatures within the building. To me the architecture of the exterior and the interior appeared humble and courageous at the same time. It combines a somewhat hand-made pop architectural stance with the poetry of a monumental craft.

What impact can the school's building have on the community in a larger sense? This school is unlike many of the other projects fostered by the Provincial Reconstruction Team (PRT), consisting of both military and civil components. The school does not refute the emergency of the local situation and at the same time intervenes consistently with the cultural and social character of this all too particular country. The building complex somehow manages to demonstrate that you can quickly create a functional architecture that has continuity not only with local, architectural and typological patterns, but also with existing traditions of structural engineering. I think it's important to work on the memories of the past that have direct and immediate implications on the present. Yet, having been in this country to deliberately observe all sorts of reconstruction works made since 2005, ranging from infrastructural to governmental approaches, I can also assure you that many things did not work out at all. Unfortunately, it is sometimes totally useless to build hardware, if the software is corrupt or damaged.

–
NAME
PAOLO FRATTER

NATIONALITY
ITALIAN

OCCUPATION
JOURNALIST

LOCATION
ROME, ITALY
–

—
'MARIA GRAZIA WOULD SURELY BE GLAD BECAUSE SHE WOULD SEE IN THIS SCHOOL A SIGN OF PEACE'
—

How are gender relations in the school dealt with? The school is opened to girls in the morning. Boys start to arrive in the early afternoon. In this way the contact between children of different genders is reduced to a minimum. This is how it works in Afghanistan, from primary school to university.

What was education like here before the school was built? The young director of the school explained how the construction of the school changed the reality of the Kosh Rod village. He said: 'Before we were in trouble. When it was possible, we used private houses as schools. But usually we met in tents or under the sun, without desks and with two or three classes all in the same place.'

Do the children enjoy their new school? The wall and the desks of the school are brand new. For these students, it is the first week in the new school. Maria is only nine years old, but she has a clear idea about her future: she wants to become a doctor and to cure the people of her village. Aurasun, one of the best students in her class, wants to become an interpreter and travel all around the world. Farisana imagines another kind of future: 'I would like to become a journalist and write articles for a newspaper like Maria Grazia Cutuli did.' The school represents Maria Grazia's image of Afghanistan, as her brother Mario Cutuli says: 'Maria Grazia would surely be glad because she would see in this school a sign of peace.'

PROJECT
SOS CHILDREN'S VILLAGES LAVEZZORIO COMMUNITY CENTER

ARCHITECT
STUDIO GANG ARCHITECTS

LOCATION
CHICAGO, ILLINOIS, USA

CHAPTER 3
REACH OUT, SPACES FOR LEARNING AND COMMUNITY

145

Studio Gang developed a way to incorporate donated materials piece-by-piece

Page
231 / 233

SOS CHILDREN'S VILLAGES LAVEZZORIO COMMUNITY CENTER
CHICAGO, ILLINOIS, USA

ONE OF AMERICA'S ONLY SOS CHILDREN'S VILLAGES, A COMMUNITY OF FOSTER FAMILIES THAT CREATE A LOVING ENVIRONMENT FOR FOSTER CHILDREN, HAS BEEN GIVEN A NEW COMMUNITY CENTRE WITH THE HELP OF STUDIO GANG. A LACK OF RESOURCES IN FACT ALLOWED THE ARCHITECTS TO COME UP WITH NOVEL APPROACHES AND CREATIVELY INCORPORATE MATERIAL DONATIONS, RESULTING IN A BEAUTIFUL STRUCTURE THAT OPENLY ADDRESSES THE CIRCUMSTANCES OF ITS OWN CREATION.

The interior space is transparent and bright

CONTEXT

Chicago's urban neighbourhoods receive little design attention compared to the city's photogenic downtown. In fact, the SOS project site is right in the middle of a virtual 'architecture desert'. This desert clearly correlates geographically with an economically-challenged African-American population on Chicago's south-west side.

SOS Children's Villages is an international non-governmental social development organization that has been active in the field of children's rights and committed to children's needs and concerns since 1949. SOS focuses on family-based, long-term care of children who can no longer grow up with their biological families.
At SOS Children's Villages and SOS Youth Facilities, they experience reliable relationships and love once again, meaning that they can recover from what they have experienced, which has often been traumatic. They grow up in a stable family environment and are supported individually until they become independent young adults.

There are approximately 500 SOS villages in a 132 countries around the world, but there are only three villages in the entire USA. And part of the reason that there are so few in this country is that it's a contrarian model of care, because it places children in individual homes, which is labour- and capital-intensive.

MISSION

The project's first goal was to bring Architecture with a capital 'A' to this under-served neighbourhood, with the belief that a well-designed civic building with a strong identity would elevate the feeling of pride for this block and become a community asset. Working with a very small budget, and asked to incorporate donated materials into the project, Studio Gang's concept was to utilize these donated materials (such as concrete) to make the building a visible beacon. Unlike the eclectic, traditional styles of the adjacent homes and businesses, the community centre projects modernity, warmth, openness and optimism.

The building needed to be an anchor that strengthened families throughout the Auburn-Gresham neighbourhood by serving the foster children from the village and members of the surrounding community – not only to meet their separate needs, but to bring them together. Foster children have specific needs: to feel safe; to be secure; to have a fun and uplifting space that encourages imagination and playfulness. In short, they need a space in which they can 'be kids'.

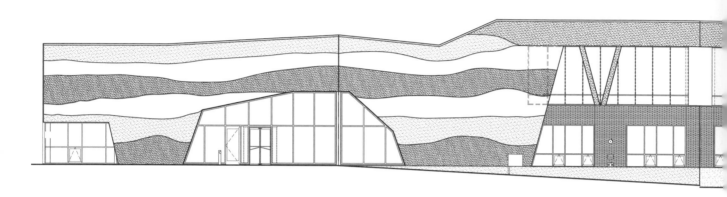

REALIZATION

Due to the project's limited funding, its realization relied on securing donated materials (many of them provided by manufacturers and builders) and incorporating them into the building's design. Studio Gang chose to treat this circumstance as an opportunity rather than a constraint, and invented a system to manage the flow of donations. Under this system, the original design maintained a series of flexible placeholder elements – from the staircase to exterior cladding – that could be reshuffled and reintegrated based on incoming donations. Each donation was treated as a variable with equal potential to affect other elements or even to suggest new donations to be sought. Working closely with general contractor Bovis Lend Lease, the team kept lists of confirmed donations, potential suppliers and donor naming opportunities, and all potential donations lived on a spreadsheet until they were integrated into the building.

—

DUE TO THE PROJECT'S LIMITED FUNDING, ITS REALIZATION RELIED ON SECURING DONATED MATERIALS AND INCORPORATING THEM INTO THE BUILDING'S DESIGN

—

Longitudinal elevation of the building

As each new donation was secured, it was examined in relation to all of its immediately adjacent parts in order to determine how best it could be incorporated. Facilitated by the use of contemporary digital tools, the analysis of combinational possibilities led the architects to discover a number of unusual and compelling results for design – the building's exterior 'strata wall' being the most visible. These surprising formal and material juxtapositions would never have been achieved had the team chosen to 'value engineer' the building (eliminating or substituting materials in favour of less expensive alternatives) rather than opening up the design to evolve according to availability. The architects' role became radically different than that of the traditional architect; instead of seeking to control and refine each design element, they became organizers of a set of chance circumstances, ready to innovate and recognize unexpected potentials.

Four lots at the end of the village are left open to make adaptations. Currently the village is in the planning phase of a Transitional Living Program, for the mature village children who will eventually go to college or get jobs.

The needs of the community were carefully considered. Counselling rooms were located on the first floor to provide security. Visibility was created between rooms through the use of glass and open floor plans in order to provide an atmosphere of transparency and safety. Imagination and playfulness were embraced, and child-friendly features were incorporated, such as the central, extra-wide 'criss cross' stair that connects the space and encourages creative movement.

The final architecture preserves and reveals the physics of a once-fluid material in the building's 'strata-wall' (so nicknamed because it resembles the geologic layers of the earth). By celebrating the cold joint rather than seeking to hide it, the building makes a clear visual statement about the donation and the construction processes that created it. The primary façade's 'stripes' help make the centre a neighbourhood icon that is aesthetically playful and open, and that welcomes village residents and the community to enter its doors.

–
NAME
TIM MCCORMICK

NATIONALITY
AMERICAN

OCCUPATION
**CHIEF EXECUTIVE OFFICER,
SOS CHILDREN'S VILLAGES ILLINOIS**

LOCATION
CHICAGO, ILLINOIS, USA
–

What does the SOS Children's Village Illinois in Chicago offer to the community? In every SOS village in the world, a community centre is integrated that acts as a social and material asset for the surrounding community. And in the Chicago centre, we've gone out into the local community and asked what would be needed, what would serve their needs the best.

How did Studio Gang get involved with this project? We were looking for three things in an architect. The first was imagination. We didn't just want to create a building; we wanted to create a centre that would spark both the children's and the community's imagination. The design needed to promote what we believe as an organization, and keep the child first. When you look at the community centre, it's designed in a very creative way, so that eyes are always directed towards the child – the child that was once neglected and forgotten needs to feel like the centre of attention.

The windows and the general transparency of the structure are really an important aspect, and the architects' imagination was responsible for this. The second thing we wanted was someone to join us as beggars! We had to go out and solicit a lot of donations. We needed someone who knew that this was really a labour of love, and who was able to help us bring in other resources. We didn't want someone who would get temperamental and give up. Case in point: the night before we opened the building, it was ten o'clock on a Sunday night, Jean, the architect, said: 'Hold on! We have to go out to get some more pillows!' So they ran to an all-night store to pick some up. Right until the end, they were working to make sure the centre had everything it needed. And so the third thing was that we wanted someone to partner with us – we weren't just looking for an architect who would build the thing and then be gone. I believe that the mindset of the village is that it's not defined by geography, it's really defined by ideologies and philosophies. It's a big thing to say, 'I will commit to this injured, unknown child, and welcome him,' to take someone in regardless of where he or she is from, and say somehow what we want with each other. A lot of architecture is built by skilled architects, but we looked more at the moral fabric of an architecture firm. We wanted someone who could understand what we are about. And we are very happy with the result.

It seems like there has been a really thorough interactive process during the design and implementation of the centre. What became an important factor in the process was the fact that we started things right before Hurricane Katrina hit. When Katrina hit, supplies and costs went up significantly in New Orleans and surrounding areas, and so some of the original designs and concepts that relied on materials coming from there couldn't be fulfilled – the dollars just weren't there. We said, 'well, wait a minute, we know that there is not enough money, but maybe we can be creative about finding other ways to get these material resources'. So we ended up taking almost a million dollars worth of donated goods for the project, including the general contractor Bovis Lend Lease, the largest contractor in the world. They are worldwide, and they were able to leverage a lot of their relationships, so everything from tiles for the floors, carpeting, the revolving door that you see at the front of the building – all were donated. That kind of work takes more time, but it also makes things affordable, and it was important for us to do it that way. It is still kind of amazing to me, how integrated and well-designed the building as a whole looks, given that the materials have come from all over. Now that the jigsaw puzzle is in place, it works very well. But that was really the architects who were part of the whole process that made sure it would work right. Take for example the façade, as it was being poured in layers, we really couldn't know how things were going to turn out. We actually had a contest in the children's homes in which they made drawings of how they thought the building would ultimately look. So if you walked into any house seven or eight or nine months before it really took its final shape, you'd see drawings of it on every refrigerator door.

NAME
ROCHELLE INGRAM

NATIONALITY
AMERICAN

OCCUPATION
CHILD AND FAMILY SERVICE COORDINATOR AT SOS CHILDREN'S VILLAGES

LOCATION
CHICAGO, ILLINOIS, USA

—

'IT'S A FULL HOUSE, AND THE CENTER IS AN ENTIRELY SELF-SUSTAINING OPERATION'

—

What is the neighbourhood like for people in your community? Auburn Gresham is a predominately African-American middle-class community. Our community is located in the 17th ward, nine miles from downtown Chicago. My family moved into Auburn Gresham, over 35 years ago hoping to raise the family here. I grew up in this community, then went away to college and returned ten years later to give back to the community that gave so much to me. That's how I got the job at SOS Children's Villages Illinois – I had the experience, but it was more the fact that I knew the area and was currently a resident. The community has its share of drug houses and gang activity. Over many years, residents have come out of their homes and spoken out against this negative activity, and they have won. At one time, the closing of commercial businesses had also devastated the area, but through the efforts of key community leaders and various Aldermen (Chicago's city council members), the businesses have begun to come back – like fast food chains, banks and grocery stores.

Do you remember what was on the lot of the community centre before it was built? The site was the home of an abandoned mattress factory. My understanding is that it all started when Mayor Daley was Principal for the Day at a Chicago public school. A child's comment about being in foster care and not seeing her siblings sparked the mayor to research the SOS Village in Lockport. From then on, the city of Chicago was on a mission to bring an SOS Village to Chicago. It was Alderman Latasha Thomas, of the 17th Ward, who steered millions in public investment to the ward, who was a pivotal aid in securing the eight-million-dollar city ante for the SOS Children's Villages Illinois' Chicago Village.

Can you describe the centre today? The structure, designed by Studio Gang, is called the Lavezzorio Community Center and is currently home to the YMCA Jenne Kenney Day Care centre, which is located on the first floor. The community room, recreation room, computer lab and administrative offices are on the second floor. I've been at the Chicago Village since October 2007, which is the same month that the centre opened its doors for service, and I'm proud to say that all the programming that is currently running on the second floor is due to my outreach efforts. We have youth programming five days a week, Tuesday through Saturday. Over 75 per cent of our programming at the centre is open to the local community. So, it's a full house and the centre is an entirely self-sustaining operation.

Beyond its physical presence, have the project and the process had wider effects on the area's residents? Yes, with the daycare downstairs opening its doors and the on-going programs for youth we have people watching us . . . In a good way.

PROJECT
**INKWENKWEZI
SECONDARY SCHOOL**

ARCHITECT
**NOERO WOLFF ARCHITECTS
WITH SONJA SPAMER
ARCHITECTS**

LOCATION
**CAPE TOWN,
SOUTH AFRICA**

▲ Increased visibility means fewer dropouts

▼ The school faces a sprawling subsidized-housing settlement

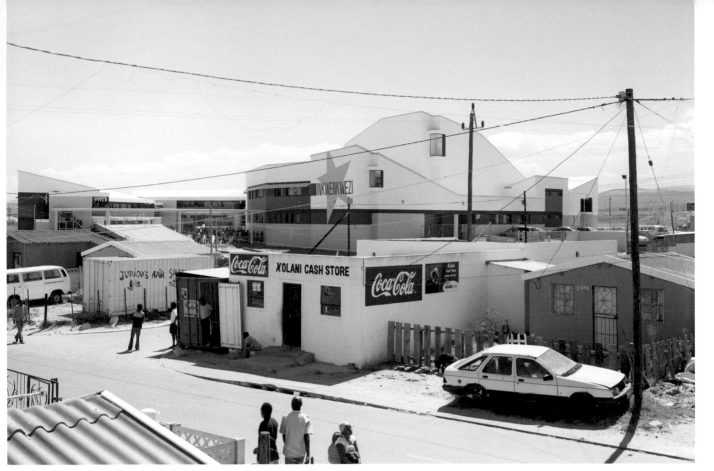

Inkwenkwezi is Xhosa for 'morning star'

Page
229 / 233
/ 242

INKWENKWEZI
SECONDARY SCHOOL
CAPE TOWN, SOUTH AFRICA

**THROUGH INTELLIGENT ARCHITECTURE WITH THE AID OF GOVERNMENTAL
AND INTERNATIONAL SUPPORT, A SCHOOL IN A POVERTY-STRICKEN
NEIGHBOURHOOD IN CAPE TOWN HAS BECOME A SAFE PLACE AND A HUB
FOR YOUTH FROM ALL OVER THE CAPE TO GAIN THE NECESSARY TOOLS
TO OVERCOME THEIR DIFFICULT SITUATIONS AND ESCAPE THE TRAPS
OF POVERTY THROUGH EDUCATION.**

CONTEXT

The Inkwenkwezi Secondary School is on a dead-end street on the periphery of a settlement next to a large sports field. The busy road to the north of the site is unsafe for pedestrians, so children enter from the quiet dead-end road. The settlement itself originated in 1996 as a neighbourhood of subsidized houses. All buildings, including stores, are in converted houses. The way a shop is differentiated from a house is through painted signage on the walls. This custom has led to a particular functional aesthetic in the area, without architects having ever been involved. In contexts such as these, radical architectural statements that make no reference to their context suggest a condemnation of local place and culture. Architecture has to make connections with the familiar world to avoid becoming inaccessible and elitist.

—

THE SCHOOL FORMS ITS OWN OUTER WALL AS A DEFENCE AGAINST THEFT AND VANDALISM

—

Since the dawn of democracy in South Africa in 1994, urgent questions have had to be asked about the role of architecture in a free society. Since political freedom does not automatically lead to the removal of the deprivations of the past, architecture must play a role in facilitating and expressing freedom. By its nature, educational facilities aim to empower the individual to have greater participation in economic, cultural and political processes. The proposed architectural corollary of this empowerment objective has been an architecture that participates in local spatial, representational and building practices, while representing optimism for a better future. A new architecture is generated out of an engagement with the familiar world.

MISSION

Through research, the architects learned that in most government schools the principal spends 60 per cent of his or her time marshalling students to classrooms. This means that the abilities of the highest-paid member of staff are completely misspent. Non-attendance is a huge problem in the South African school system. The need to get students to class efficiently and the ability to survey recreation areas from a central position

had a great bearing on the school's morphology. The second goal was to give the school a relationship to the area that it is part of, which is devoid of any other public buildings. This was done through engaging the tradition of wall decoration to delineate function. The third issue was that the school needed to function as a community facility — capable of transforming into a church, a wedding venue or a musical performance place. Since this project was presented in an open public tender where the lowest tender got the job, the building had to employ fairly conventional technologies to ensure that the proposed design would be realized. The challenge was to create a new architecture out of conventional materials.

REALIZATION

The location of the building at the edge of the settlement on a sloping lot was taken advantage of in order to develop a piece of civic architecture that distinguishes itself from the residential fabric around it with its scale and sculptural form. The main hall rises to a tall corner, which is exaggerated by vertical fluting and an attractive window. The entrance façade in conjunction with the hall and the library and administration block forms a syncopated profile in a composite façade. The entrance to the school is along a ramp, which cuts through this façade. Despite its monumentality, the school participates in the visual and building culture of the surrounding area. Furthermore, the use of conventional building materials and techniques allowed extensive participation of the local community in the building process. Basic concrete work, masonry, plastering and painting could all be undertaken by members of the community. Participation in the building process created many local jobs, and gave the community a sense of ownership.

The school forms its own outer wall as a defence against theft and vandalism. All access points and recreation areas are within the safety of the entrance gates. Attendance has been raised via the creation of a single central courtyard that can be surveyed from all sides. At the school's previous temporary location, the pass rate at the end of the school year was 40 per cent. After the new building was completed, this number rose to 70 per cent within the first year. The main courtyard of the school makes a space where children can be protected from strong winds and from crime in the area. The edges of the court are planted with trees and have several level changes and benches to allow children to each find their own space within the larger area. The facilities have been designed to allow the school to serve and generate income for the broader community.

▶ View of the interior courtyard

NAME
SHARON SEQAMATA

NATIONALITY
SOUTH AFRICAN

OCCUPATION
SCHOOL SECRETARY/ADMINISTRATOR

LOCATION
CAPE TOWN, SOUTH AFRICA

–

What do you do for the school?
I've been the school secretary for eight years. I have known the building from its very beginning to how it is now.

And how was that process?
The process was long and tedious. The ground the school is built on was mostly water, so the foundation had to be very strong, which took a long time.

Did people from the community help in the building and designing process? Yes, they were all involved in the building of the school. They taught unemployed people the necessary skills and then employed them in construction. We are very proud of the building. It looks very beautiful.

How does it relate to the other buildings in the area? It actually looks like a supermarket! When they were still building, people kept asking when the supermarket would open. Now they are amazed that it's actually a school and not a shopping centre.

And what is the demographic like? What is the area like? The school has 1,168 pupils and more than 30 educators. Surrounding the school, there are about 3,000 brick houses and a lot of shacks, or temporary housing. Near the school there is a lady who runs an organization to help people who are unemployed. Students who don't have parents go to her also, and she helps them get uniforms, school supplies and food. The school also has a food plan, which is supported by the government. Most of our pupils use the food plan. They eat their lunches at half past ten in the morning, and then they won't eat again until the following day, because most of their parents don't work. We have a lot of kids who come to school because it's the only place where they will get a meal.

What else goes on in the school? It is also used sometimes for weddings and performances, right?
Yes! I think two or three weddings took place there. The pupils do fundraising in the school, and there are church events there too. When the library opened up they had a huge function in the school, it was like a show. We also rent out the classrooms and the hall to generate money for the community.

Is the shape of the school important? The courtyard? Oh yes, the courtyard is shaped like a triangle, so wherever you stand you can actually see the courtyard and you can see what is happening there. You can't enter the school building unless you go through the courtyard.

Are most of the teachers local people? No, only two are three are from the community. And most of our students actually come from the Eastern Cape – they come to the school because they love it so much. They even changed the school uniform colours to match the school building: mustard and baby blue.

What do the children who go to the school do after they graduate?
Some work for the Chevron refinery, others go to work for a chemical company. Some study, some practice law, some are nurses, some are accountants, some are designers. A lot of them are now teachers themselves. One is even an architect!

What do you think is the main challenge that the school now faces? The main challenge is that we are in a red zone, which is a dangerous area. In January, one of our pupils passed away in the school foyer, because he had been stabbed outside. He ran into the school and died in the foyer. Another challenge that we have is student pregnancy. Many of the students' parents are unemployed. Many don't even live with their parents – they stay with relatives who don't care about them. So the only way for the girls to get money is to have sugar daddies. And the sugar daddies will tell them to open up their legs before they can get money, which is how they get pregnant. Drug use is another big challenge.

What can you do to combat these things? Has the school become a safe place for people to go and get help? Yes and no. Yes, because they know that if they need help, they can go to certain educators and tell them the problem. And the educator goes to the department and gets a social worker to get involved. But if the pupil needs help fast, right now, he or she has to go to the lady who runs the organization next door, because she can offer immediate help. For example, we had a problem with a pupil last weekend. He had been sent from his parents' house to stay with his uncle, who said that he would help buy uniforms and books. But then when the child came to Cape Town, the uncle changed his mind and told him to go away. So the child had no place to go or anything to eat. He was always happy at school, but when it came time for him to go home, he was despondent. Finally, he spoke to his teacher, who spoke to us, and then we went to the lady next door, because this child needed help immediately. She gave him a place to sleep. Unfortunately I don't know what has happened to the child now, because someone told his uncle that he had spoken to us, and we haven't seen him since then.

To really help the students, we would need to start a hostel. Then they wouldn't have to sleep with their sugar daddies, or their boyfriends, or at their classmates' houses. But to have a hostel on school premises we would have to talk to the government.

It is really a luxury to be able to go to school. Yes. Our educators are trying their best. Our principal is giving all the time, his utmost. Everybody, even the administrators, we want to help the pupils. Educators will be there at seven o'clock in the morning and go home at eight in the evening. And they don't get extra money for what they are doing. That is how dedicated we are to the pupils.

Some who have matriculated three years ago still come back to school to say thank you. There is one guy who is in jail in the Eastern Cape, who actually wrote a letter to us saying that he wants to continue his schooling. Even though he went back to the Eastern Cape and he did something wrong, he still contacted us for help.

So you are making some progress. It's slow and difficult, but there is progress. What else can you say about the school building itself? At the moment we've got four or six labs, which are being used to the full. Especially the life sciences lab, which is also called biology – that lab is working at 100 per cent. Our two computer labs are also working. So, our labs are being fully utilized. The only complaint I have about the school is the noise in the hall. Every time you talk there is an echo in the hall. That's the only thing that we can say is a negative. But everything else about the building is positive. If only someone could take that echo out

NAME
TEMBUXOLO KUTU

NATIONALITY
SOUTH AFRICAN

OCCUPATION
EDUCATOR

LOCATION
CAPE TOWN, SOUTH AFRICA
–

Where do the school's students come from? What is the town like? The Du Noon community where the school is situated is poverty-stricken. A number of parents do not have stable jobs and as a result live in shacks. The community faces an HIV and AIDS pandemic and some homes are actually run by children. Pupils come to school without having eaten. The community's social ills spill over into life at school.

Where was class held before the school was built? The school did not have a permanent structure before, just a temporary place that was extremely cold in winter and extremely hot in summer. There were no learning facilities such as laboratories, computers and a library. The building started after the community pressured the government to provide us with a school, and then the architects were appointed.

How was your experience with the architects? How was the plan conceived? The architects consulted with the community, and we visited other school buildings for ideas. But they designed a unique building, and they took some suggestions I gave them, like creating an enclosed structure that could be easily monitored to ensure the safety of pupils and teachers. Local labourers built the school, and a community member acted as liaison between the community and the building contractor regarding some issues.

How have things been since the school was built? The architects have visited the school on a number of occasions and they have also donated a garage building plan for later use. The community is still excited about the building and proud of the school. Community member groups are permitted to use the school for their meetings and faith meetings. The project provided a source of income to some members and there is a sense of ownership because they were involved in the building process. The school's programming, however, is not yet self-sufficient.

PROJECT
OLD MARKET LIBRARY

ARCHITECT
**TYIN TEGNESTUE WITH
KASAMA YAMTREE**

LOCATION
BANGKOK, THAILAND

Raised platforms pre-empt annual floods

Page
230 / 233 /
236

OLD MARKET LIBRARY
BANGKOK, THAILAND

A LIBRARY IN THAILAND EXPLORES LOCAL INVOLVEMENT IN ORDER TO ADDRESS SOCIAL AND ECOLOGICAL ISSUES THROUGH USE OF LOCAL MATERIALS, LABOR, AND COOPERATION.

The original market building is 100 years old

CONTEXT

Min Buri's Old Market Community was once the area's commercial centre, but a fire in the late 1990s caused the market activities to move across the canal. In recent years, the community has diminished from a lively place into an almost slum-like area. Land rights in Min Buri are uncertain, and partly because of this the inhabitants are reluctant to invest in their houses. Additionally, community members generally have no job security, and have limited access to services like health, water, sanitation, housing and education. Even though many of the people in Min Buri make an income, the cost of living is rising rapidly as the population of Bangkok's urban area grows and density makes accommodation scarce. The urban poor in areas like Min Buri are in many regards a group excluded from social and humanitarian support systems.

MISSION

For TYIN it was not only the creation of a physical library that was important, but also that the efforts made would affect the Min Buri community on a larger scale. Through the use of local, inexpensive materials, the architects wanted to demonstrate that creating

The architects learned a lot from their first project in Thailand, an orphanage in Noh Bo, where it proved that good ideas sometimes do not work well in practice at all and an intense understanding of local conditions is necessary.

inhabitable community spaces is possible for residents to do according to their own initiative in the future. The aim of the library project is to create energy and excitement in the neighbourhood and teach useful skills that can contribute to further positive development.

The team wanted to involve the inhabitants actively throughout the whole process. Initially, the community's needs were assessed through regular meetings. The meetings' activities ranged from drawing and building models to picking up garbage at the playground. Aside from getting to know people, TYIN hoped to create awareness about the challenges that the community faces and gain a deeper understanding of the situation people are living in. As part of a survey, area residents were interviewed about their views on the community's past, present and future.

REALIZATION

The Old Market Library was built in a 100-year-old market building in a 3 x 9 m area, with a back yard facing a small canal. The roof and walls of the original structure were in poor condition, so it was important that new elements in the building supported themselves.

The high ceiling in the main room allowed for the contraction of a loft area that creates more intimate areas both above and below. The library was divided into two zones along its length; on one side, visitors can pass through the building and look at books on the wall, while the other side is for reading and other calm activities. Beyond the main room is a smaller space called the study, and in the back yard, a pergola was constructed to protect against the blazing sun. Jasmine and climbing plants in large ceramic pots will eventually grow to further shade the space.

One of the community's main challenges is the annual flooding during the rainy season, during which water can rise up to 50 cm above floor level. To retain the water would have been very challenging, so the solution was to instead elevate certain zones to ensure that the library would be usable throughout the flooded periods. Concrete sidewalls and aired connections prevent humidity and rot in the wooden constructions. A very important principle for the project was the utilization of used or local materials. The bookshelves are made of wooden boxes from one of CASE's earlier projects, and the cladding is put together using old and decayed wooden pieces found in the immediate surroundings.

—

ON ONE SIDE VISITORS PASS THROUGH THE BUILDING AND LOOK AT BOOKS ON THE WALL, THE OTHER SIDE IS FOR READING AND OTHER CALM ACTIVITIES

—

The constructive materials, which had higher quality requirements, were bought at a local second-hand wood shop. It was not always easy to get everyone involved, especially adults. But as the project became more tangible, a regular group formed that worked with TYIN every day. Through this process the workers became personally attached to the project, which suggests success for the library in the long term.

▼ Several gathering places provide distinct areas for different activities

► Min Buri's children use the library for dance rehearsals

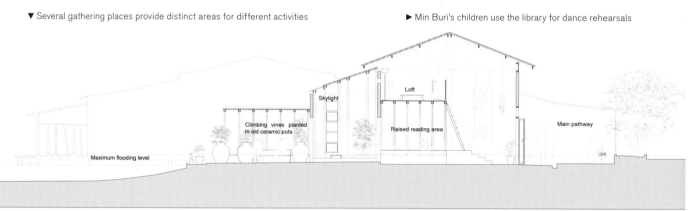

SECTION 1:100

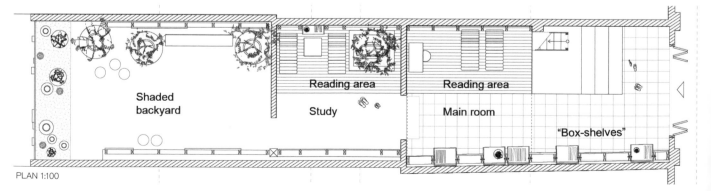

PLAN 1:100

–
NAME
KASAMA YAMTREE

NATIONALITY
THAI

OCCUPATION
ARCHITECT

LOCATION
BANGKOK, THAILAND
–

How did this project come about? Working as an architect around the corner from the Old Market Library, I passed by almost every day. This is how I learned a lot of stories about that district and the old market that used to be there. What attracted me at first to this run-down neighbourhood is its architecture, which is a unique Chinese type of shop-house that you cannot find anywhere else in Thailand. Since I didn't know anybody there, I basically spent half a year just walking around, going into the community and talking to the people, getting to know them, getting them familiar with me. I think building up confidence and trust is an essential part of any type of process.

What was the eventual jumping-off point for the project to start? I was kind of lucky, because I was talking to a loaning company called GE Money, which was interested in doing a corporate social responsibility project. They were basically asking me if I had a project that could be implemented immediately that they could get involved in. So, I just started having normal community meetings, and then started asking people if they would be interested in creating a project as a starting point to start changing their own environment. The housing conditions and the living conditions were not very good at that time. There were teenagers killing each other and people selling drugs on the streets. In addition there was a great insecurity about land ownership, as most of the residents used to rent their living spaces from the Ministry of Treasury, but at one point the ministry abruptly stopped collecting the rent. As a result people got quite scared about being expelled from their homes over night. Therefore no one in the community wanted to change anything to make their neighbourhood better, since they assumed they were going to be expelled eventually anyway. I thought that if they put some effort into changing the environment, maybe they could use the change as a tool to show the landowners that they were capable of taking care of the property, and they could stay there.

How did you then get the people involved in the project? With a group of mainly kids and a few adults, we started to build a playground in an empty lot where there had once been a market that had burned down. It was left abandoned after the fire, there were broken bricks and glass all over for 11 years without change. It was really dangerous for kids, because lots of them don't wear shoes. We started on this area because we thought that the children could benefit most. Apart from that, the area is actually in the middle of two main roads and people from outside the community cross this area to go to another road. So it actually benefits not just the community people but the whole public. We thought this could be quite a nice area to start out with. When we eventually received the funding from GE Money, we spent weeks just cleaning the area, and we finished the whole playground in two months. At that time, I thought it was really successful, because it was not just about changing the environment, but about getting people interested in changing their own environment. In that way, it led to the library project. If I hadn't done the playground project, I wouldn't have been able to start the library project at all, because no one would have believed in changing anything in that area. So, when TYIN came, I thought that the people in the area were ready to do something more. At first I was interested in doing some house renovation project, but I couldn't really just go into anyone's private house. But there's no conflict if you do something in a public area, especially when people start believing in you, that you are actually bringing out some positive things. After about two months of doing some designing with the kids and adults, they all agreed to have a library. And then we thought that maybe moving from outdoors to indoors could be quite interesting to show that one shop house that was very old could actually be renovated without too much money. We got a free shop house from an old woman who had been watching us while we were brainstorming and making designs.

It's amazing how the project started by getting the community involved and getting them to trust you and believe that they could do it themselves. It seems like half of the battle was convincing people that improvement was worthwhile. Yes, indeed. I think the key to the entire process was the fact that I didn't rush anything at any point. Instead I tried to spend time with the community. Nothing was rushed, so they were quite relaxed. We didn't actually wait until every single person agreed to help, but once we got started, other people would see things change a bit, and that's why more and more started coming in. Now there is even a permanent group trying to change things inside the community. Recently, they told me that they were really happy about the library and the playground, because they are actually facing and seeing each other more often. It has developed into a popular area for adults and children to come to meet. Interestingly enough, before, people in the community didn't really have any communal space whatsoever. Now some of the residents are trying to create activities, like one activity each month, to bring the children out to play. One guy told me that lots of kids in the community leave the area to go play computer games, but now, on activity nights, only a few of them leave.

How did the collaboration with TYIN architects work out? I was trying to get people to participate. And I was helping TYIN collaborate with the people in the community. When TYIN came I told them that I wasn't just going to let them build something and then leave, because that is not going to create any positive change. There are some companies here who want to do this corporate social responsibility type of thing, where they just look for communities to throw some money at and then get out quickly. That's not what we were after. So I told them, you have to participate in the whole process, you have to learn to design with kids, you have to learn to design with the community so that you understand what kind of things they really want. I had a group of interested people already from working on the playground that they could use as a support system for making something more. TYIN were really interested in this, because it could be quite different from the project they did in the north before. We started by spending a lot of time on the design by just talking with the adults and kids in the community.

And then when building started, it was really surprising that there were some new faces coming in and out, not just the original playground group. People would come and swap places during the day. TYIN was on-site for the whole process. I think they spent like a month and a half designing and then a month building.

How did the design of the library address the local conditions and what special considerations had to be made? First of all, we had to face the challenge of the rainy season, because the library is located in the middle of two water gates and gets heavily flooded once a year. Secondly, we had to make sure that someone would take care of the place after the building process was finished. Because we didn't want to build it if no one was going to maintain it. Everybody in the group had to agree to take care of it. Two positive side effects were also that the landowners actually stopped collecting the rent in this area, and that one of the adjacent residents spontaneously agreed to connect the library with his private electricity and water supply.

Afterwards we even got some money from the community to pay for it. After all, the entire community agreed to take care of the library. After the experience of building the playground together they were already confident that they could really have a positive impact on their own community. The kids, for example, make sure that everyone entering the library takes off their shoes and if they see someone still wearing shoes, they will start shouting 'go, go, go, get out, get out!' They really feel that they own the place. It is also interesting to see how the library is used as much more than a space for reading. It is also used for dance rehearsals, as all the children in this community really enjoy dancing. Since they don't have space to dance when it rains, they use the library for rehearsing. The library was created for the eyes of both outsiders and insiders. The community people are more careful now because they could lose what they have gained. And everybody is watching it in this community.

—
'I THINK THE KEY TO THE ENTIRE PROCESS WAS THE FACT THAT I DIDN'T RUSH ANYTHING AT ANY POINT. INSTEAD I TRIED TO SPEND TIME WITH THE COMMUNITY'
—

PROJECT
AHMED BABA CENTRE

ARCHITECT
**DHK ARCHITECTS
AND TWOTHINK**

LOCATION
TIMBUKTU, MALI

TESTIFY!
THE CONSEQUENCES OF ARCHITECTURE

170

AHMED BABA CENTRE
TIMBUKTU, MALI

A SOPHISTICATED ARCHIVE LIBRARY IN THE CENTRE OF TIMBUKTU'S HISTORICAL DISTRICT PROVIDES A PLACE FOR THE PRESERVATION OF LONG-NEGLECTED MANUSCRIPTS AND INVITES A RE-EXAMINATION OF AFRICAN HISTORY.

CONTEXT

Timbuktu's lively streets are packed with pedestrians, donkeys and the odd car meandering through the dense and slow-moving network. The city has a high poverty level, with a working population of only 20 per cent, yet there is an atmosphere of coexistence, particularly apparent when walking the intricate network of streets. This is in stark contrast with Mali's capital city Bamako, whose streets are vehicle-dominated, making urban life chaotic and unmanageable. Bamako's urban sprawl is the result of modern urban planning ideals, where long highways connect remote zones, and the car becomes the most important mode of transport. The results of such planning principles are fallow pieces of useless land that segregate the city. Timbuktu, on the other hand, closely resembles the European 'ring road' model, in which car use is largely restricted to the outer and inner ring of streets and only permeates the pedestrian realm at certain points.

The sophistication and complexity of Timbuktu's urban pattern was the focus for the Ahmed Baba architectural team. The Ahmed Baba site is located at the junction of the 'old' and the 'new' parts of the city, and is adjacent to the famous Sankore Mosque, which marks a pivotal point in the metropolis. Three main arterial roads lead to the site, making it an important centre of activity.

MISSION

The Ahmed Baba Centre in Timbuktu has the unique mission of preserving and presenting the ancient written treasures that testify to Africa's intellectual past, challenging the common notion that the continent has only an oral tradition. Manuscripts date from as early as the twelfth century and are mainly written in Arabic, with a few exceptions in local languages. They cover a broad range of subjects from history, theology, law and

When South Africa's former President, Thabo Mbeki, visited Mali in 2001, he declared the documents to be among the continent's 'most important cultural treasures' and promised to help conserve them as part of his vision of an 'African renaissance'. The new centre has been completely paid for by the South African Government.

astronomy to medicine. In addition, factual documents such as letters, journals and legal papers give an insight into Timbuktu's society and history. These delicate books from pre-colonial Muslim Africa are highly endangered by the climate and insects. While there are currently around 80 private libraries in Timbuktu, often the owners don't have the means or expertise to ensure the preservation of their manuscripts. The first efforts to save them were made in 1970 at UNESCO's initiative. The IHERI-AB (Institute des Hautes Etudes et de Recherche Islamique Ahmed Baba) was established 30 years later as an independent institute of higher learning, with the legal and financial framework to assure the 'restoration and conservation, scientific exploitation and dissemination of the manuscripts in possession while also offering services to private collectors and owners'.

REALIZATION

Ahmed Baba's physical plan was inspired by Timbuktu's layout. 'The first take was just looking at the urban planning of Timbuktu, which had a sporadic and organic growth,' explains project architect Andre Spies. 'It's a straightforward approach: a few buildings grouped around a courtyard and walkways, and that is pretty much the way in which Timbuktu grew as well.' Four separate blocks defined programmatically as the archive, restoration area, research spaces and auditorium are spread along a patio. An open amphitheatre makes the connection with the surrounding urban square, drawing in the public from the street. The archive, which holds over 30,000 items, is housed in a basement to lower dependency on air conditioning and electricity. Covered open spaces link all the enclosed buildings to create free airflow and natural ventilation, and internal walkways replicate the patterns of movement in Timbuktu's city streets. It was important to the South African

◄ The Ahmed Baba Centre will house over 30,000 manuscripts

▲ The centre is located between the 'old' and 'new' parts of the city

▼ Nearby is the famous Sankore Mosque

IN TIMBUKTU'S CHALLENGING CONTEXT, THE NEW AHMED BABA CENTRE ASSUMES THE DIFFICULT ROLE OF A SUBTLE MEDIATOR BETWEEN DIFFERENT SPACES, DIFFERENT TIMES AND DIFFERENT WORLDS

architects that the local workforce in Mali be used for the construction of the archive. During the process, the South African technical team travelled to Timbuktu regularly, and a team of ten South Africans remained in Timbuktu for two full years.

The architecture of the centre relates to the site's interstitial zone, in that it is a combination of sun-baked mud bricks reminiscent of the 'old' city and off-shutter concrete reminiscent of the 'new' city. These two substances form the main structural materials and are tectonically separated by glass. Together they create an obvious contrast between old and new techniques, which in turn relate directly to the area. In Timbuktu's challenging context, the new Ahmed Baba Centre assumes the difficult role of a subtle mediator between different spaces, different times and different worlds.

Temperature and humidity must be carefully regulated to preserve the ancient manuscripts

NAME
ANDRE SPIES

NATIONALITY
SOUTH AFRICAN

OCCUPATION
ARCHITECT

LOCATION
CAPE TOWN, SOUTH AFRICA
–

We are curious to know what has been going on with the building since it was finished. It seems like it has actually been a complicated transition to becoming a functional, useful archive. From my understanding, since we handed the building over, it's been quite a lengthy process. First of all, they had to allow the building to cure properly before the manuscripts could be moved in. And then they decided to build a wall around the centre because they felt it was too open. A lot of things have been changing . . . I think the South African side doesn't really have a good idea of what's going on. There's definitely a political side to it that is quite difficult to address. Because it's basically up to their government to sort of take it over now and run with it.

What is going on politically? That is a very difficult thing for me to comment on. I would come across as quite biased. I have my own view of how things were done and I don't really understand the role-playing of the two

countries involved, South Africa and Mali. I will say that it didn't happen as fast as I would have liked it to, but last I heard, it seemed like things were finally moving a little bit. With an archive, or any government building, it's not just a smooth transition . . . all of us can see that it's not just a matter of finishing the building in blind moves and 'off you go', like it would be with commercial building. It certainly took a long time to negotiate things, especially regarding the interplay of different government departments. Other than that I can't really say much more. And I don't think there is anybody on our team who could actual say more.

How did you as architects get involved in the first place? How we got involved? It's not really one of those fancy stories. The company I was working for at the time was involved in construction of a large commercial building in Cape Town. That project had quite a few political connections, and somebody thought it would be a good project for the South African government to sponsor. They jumped on it, and decided to put together a professional team for the project.

This sounds very straightforward. We have been told that the manuscripts are not actually being housed in the archive yet. Is that related to the political situation? I think it is. The last time that I was there, which was probably a good seven or eight months ago, we did a couple more tests on the humidity and the temperature in the basement archive. It is absolutely imperative that the temperature and humidity is constant, to preserve the manuscripts. It was nearly okay, but the humidity level was slightly too high. Those manuscripts are so used to a very low relative humidity percentage that it would have been disastrous to move them over without the correct levels. The archives are below ground to

keep the manuscripts cool without air conditioning, but the curing takes so much longer down there. The cement has to dry out for a long time before it's ready. And on top of that, there are political issues as well.

Were you expecting all of these modifications before? All the construction downstairs was very wet. We used concrete block and a cement floor with piling on top, which is a process that involves a lot of water, and it is all below ground, so evaporation is slow. Even though we've been running the air conditioning constantly to try to get rid of the water, it's taking quite a long time. And besides that, our electrical and mechanical engineer has had to go back two or three times. He might have returned recently. They had a lot of problems with the air conditioning. The need for it has been reduced substantially because the archive is underground, but the temperature still needs to be maintained at a constant level.

There is a long-term maintenance issue then? Yes. I think there is one thing I can add as an overall comment, just from an architectural perspective. Sometimes, it's quite difficult when you agree on something and then you sort of run with it. In retrospect I almost wonder if the building – even though I tried my best to make it fit into its surroundings and still bring that modern element in – I wonder if it's not possibly almost too big for a country like that. It's quite an amazing asset, but at the same time it's also a liability.

It's a liability? How so? Well, it's a large building that needs to be maintained. Even though I think it's relatively low-maintenance as far as buildings go, it's still a large space. You've got to keep it clean and hire people to work there. And the feeling I've got now is that the Malian government doesn't really push a lot of resources towards those sorts of things. I think this is something that you need to keep in the back of your mind when you are designing things in developing countries – even though South Africa is also a developing country. You really have to look at the economic structure of the thing, as well as how it is going to hold up in the long run; how will it operate from the beginning?

One of our main interests is to understand how to reach a level of self-sustainability and a life for the building beyond the structure itself. This, of course, requires institutional support, a constant infusion of funds, personnel . . . lots of things make a facility run after it's been built. Exactly! For this building, it's almost like you need a marketing team that can market it to the international market, and convey how important it is. It could really be marketed to increase the tourism industry in Timbuktu – which is kind of a dying industry right now. I think if I ever were to get involved in something similar again, I would like to have a strong basis for those things from the beginning.

It's hard to know where the architect's role is in this complex framework. Yes, it is! But we can't shy away from that sort of anthropomorphic side of our work, even though we're not qualified in it. With experience, one can gain that sort of sensitivity over time. That attitude is really what constitutes sustainability in my opinion, much more than just using 'green materials'.

–
NAME
SEYDOU TRAORE

NATIONALITY
MALIAN

OCCUPATION
TRANSLATOR

LOCATION
TIMBUKTU, MALI
–

What is your relationship with the centre? For this project I worked with the South African architects as an on-site translator during the building process from 2007 to 2009. After the building process was finished, I got involved once more with the centre last year, when a South African politician asked me to be his guide during his visit in town. As I took him around the building, I think he was not very happy with the state the building was in, as there were minor visible damages like cracks in the walls and parts of the ceiling coming down. So, I was in charge of hiring some workers do go and fix these little remedial works.

Has the building undergone major changes since its completion? No, the main shape of the building has not been changed, but as I said some technical details had to be altered. Like the state of the ceiling for example. If you put the plaster on the ceiling and then paint it, the ceiling won't bind to the plaster, because it's too smooth, so you have to open it and chop at it.

Or when the wood and the cement won't stick together, you need to add chicken wire to bind them together. And if you put cement inside, and clay outside, then it doesn't bind. There are lots of little technical questions that you simply can't consider beforehand, if you don't come from here. You don't know how much cement to use, you don't know how it will react eventually here. This is probably due to the quality of the sand in Timbuktu, which is different than in other places. If you come from outside, you just don't know these things. Also, if it rains, the water will enter the buildings. So if you build before the rainy season, you might not expect water to ever come in your building, and you will have to adapt your building slightly after the first heavy rain. But this is normal. One learns in the process of time how to best strengthen the building.

How does the centre relate to its surroundings? It fits in with the other buildings here, because we have a particular way of building with mud, cement and traditional limestone. The Ahmed Baba Centre looks like it is in the middle of the city, but it is not anymore, since the city is getting bigger and bigger every year. The centre now literally bridges the gap between the old and the new parts of the city.

How is the centre being used? We are having a lot of meetings with the various politicians and with the local people, as we are saying that it's necessary that people go to the building and really commence working there. Sure, a few people are already there, but we are urging them to start using the facilities properly. All that needs to be done is to move all of the manuscripts and the management from the old centre to the new building. That's all. Hopefully it will happen soon.

PROJECT
INUJIMA ART PROJECT:
SEIRENSHO

ARCHITECT
**HIROSHI SAMBUICHI
ARCHITECTS**

LOCATION
INUJIMA, JAPAN

The museum is entirely energy neutral

Page
229 / 233

INUJIMA ART PROJECT
INUJIMA, JAPAN

AN ENERGY-NEUTRAL ART MUSEUM IN A CONVERTED COPPER REFINERY FLOURISHES ON AN ISOLATED ISLAND IN JAPAN'S SETO SEA, MESHING WITH ITS ENVIRONMENT AND INVITING VISITORS TO GAIN A NEW AWARENESS ABOUT THE NATURAL WORLD AROUND US.

View of artist Yukinori Yanagi's installation *Hero Dry Cell / Solar Rock*

CONTEXT

Inujima is an isolated island in Japan's Seto Inland Sea. Orignally, Inujima flourished as a granite quarry. A copper refinery was constructed on the site in 1909 but shut down after ten years. Since then it has remained basically untouched for almost 100 years, vacant except for the ruins of abandoned quarries and refinery plants.

After a century of disuse, the property was purchased by the wealthy businessman Soichiro Fukutake, who wanted to rehabilitate the site and build a museum that would have minimal impact on the environment. He commissioned architect Hiroshi Sambuichi to design the new complex and conceptual artist Yukinori Yanagi to design permanent installations in the space. The task for the architect was to create a completely natural, energy-driven, air conditioned place for art that consumes no fossil energy resources whatsoever.

Dealing with what is already there is probably one of the greatest challenges for the building industry today. But as this project shows, the change from an industrial to an increasingly pluralistic service and information society has opened up new possibilities for using the old and dated infrastructures in fresh and surprising ways.

MISSION

From the outset, the architect perceived all the existing materials on the island as regenerative resources – including the architecture of the ruins, waste materials and natural environment itself. The new museum, he felt, had to be in complete symbiosis with the environment and part of the natural cycle of growth, weathering and decay. The actual structure of the museum was planned according to the limitations and possibilities of the landscape and the available materials. The architectural proposal was to control the art museum's environment using only sustainable natural energies. 'Our idea is completely different from existing natural high-tech energy applications, such as solar panels or wind power, and even rejects the idea of converting the energy into electricity,' says Sambuichi. 'This is because we believe that the true meaning of the term "sustainable environment" can only be realized when the system is used in tandem with perpetual natural activities.'

◄ The disused factory chimney is a central element of the architecture

▲ Inujima hopes to bring visitors to a better understanding of environmental cycles

REALIZATION

Sambuichi chose to build within the ruins of the refinery between the tallest of the five defunct smokestacks and the remains of the brick factory structure that spread out towards the sea. Since the island is mainly granite, Sambuichi decided to use its heat capacity effectively. His team analysed Karami bricks (a by-product of the copper refinery), and slag (leftover waste from the metal smelting process), and discovered their useful heat properties. It was decided to use the recycled bricks and slag in combination with natural granite for the construction of the floor and walls as heat-conducting materials. Steel, weathered and oxidized to represent the high-iron content of the island geology, was chosen as another main construction element. The roof is timber and glass.

Although the chimney stacks are no longer functional in their original sense, they still create a chimney effect whereby air is sucked in at the bottom and blown out of the top. The architect adapted one of the chimneys as part of an interesting environmental control mechanism for modulating internal temperature; the chill from underground cools the air of the Earth Gallery, the sun warms

the Sun Gallery, and in the Chimney Hall, the sun's energy combines with the updraft from the chimney as an additional source of heat. The two heat levels are blended together and controlled in a third space, the Energy Hall. The Energy Hall maintains the same temperature and humidity throughout the year.
The twisting corridor and the chimney system encourage air circulation. When walking through the space, visitors can feel both the cooling air and the earth's heat.
The art in the Chimney Hall is kinetic, which allows visitors to experience the mechanism of the natural convection visually and understand how the chimney works.

The energy consumption of traditional buildings such as art museums increases in step with the number of visitors. On Inujima, sewage from the museum toilets is converted into fertilizer for the island's plants. The hope is that the plants outside the structure will flourish as the number of visitors increases. Making humans part of the original environmental cycle is part of a realistic and sustainable long-term view.

MALE 65 YEARS OLD /
FEMALE 77 YEARS OLD

NATIONALITY
JAPANESE

OCCUPATION
**CHAIRMAN OF THE NEIGHBORHOOD
ASSOCIATION/
PART-TIME STAFF**

LOCATION
INUJIMA, JAPAN

—

'THE INUJIMA ART PROJECT AIMS TO BE A REFUGE TO MEDITATE UPON AND RE-EVALUATE JAPANESE LIFE AND CULTURE AND THE RAPID MODERNIZATION PROCESS AFTER THE SECOND WORLD WAR'

—

What was the site like before the Inujima Art Project began?

When the granite quarry and the copper refinery were still running, more than 3,000 people lived here. But after the refinery was closed almost 100 years ago, the population rapidly declined. The young generation moved to the mainland and the remaining population was reduced to approximately 60 people. In 2001 the site was slated for use as a medical waste dump, but was then saved thanks to Soichiro Fukutake, who bought the site of the former refinery with the plan to eventually start an artistic project that would allow the Japanese to reflect upon their own industrial heritage. Fukutake wanted to create something new based on the idea of creatively adapting what is already there, and in the process got involved with architect Hiroshi Sambuichi, about whom he read in an architecture magazine. In combining the work of Sambuichi, who's known for his environmentally aware use of renewable energy sources, and that of contemporary artists Yukinori Yanagi, whose work explores themes relating to broader issues about Japanese identity within social or national constructs, the Inujima Art Project aims to be a refuge to meditate upon and re-evaluate Japanese life and culture and the rapid modernization process after the Second World War.

Has the project been well-received by community members?

At present about 15 people, which is actually more than 30 per cent of the population of the island, are employed in planting, daily cleaning, facilities management and the museum café. We deliberately try to include the inhabitants as much as possible and organize various events together. Recently, we planted about 30 cherry blossom seedlings. There's generally a great hospitality towards us. Our staff is also regularly supplied with fresh fish and vegetables by the islanders.

Is the project self-sustaining at this point?

By now, we have more than 50,000 visitors annually! In particular young people in their twenties and thirties. They come to learn about Japan's industrial heritage and experience the creative interaction of contemporary architecture, art and environmental awareness. The museum fully embodies the spirit of a recycling society and provides practical ideas on how to productively deal with such former industrial regions. What is great is that our facility does not use any electrical energy for air conditioning inside the building, as it's constructed to keep a stable temperature throughout the year. Moreover, we introduced an environmental system that purifies sewage from the building by biological filters. This purified water is used for the nourishment of the citrus plants on the site.

Has the project impacted the community in a larger sense?

Yes, a lot. Interestingly enough and despite the already small number of inhabitants on Inujima, some of the Islanders are starting to meet and engage with one another again as part of the team here at the museum. It's also nice to see that a cross-generational exchange is happening between our staff members and the elderly locals, who teach them local recipes and menus from Inujima. And with the large amount of visitors and increasing naval transport activity, the overall communication with the people from the mainland is evidently increasing. People from the mainland are even thinking about opening a café here.

NAME
IWAN BAAN

NATIONALITY
DUTCH

OCCUPATION
PHOTOGRAPHER

LOCATION
THE NETHERLANDS

When did you first visit Inujima?

The first time I went there was about two years ago, I was invited to the opening of the museum by Sambuichi. But since then I've been back a couple of times – I went just two months ago, because I'm currently working on a book about all the neighbouring islands and the many newly commissioned works of art, buildings and landscape designs in the surrounding area. What fascinates me about these islands is that for all the visitors it's this big experience. They have to travel to this island far away from Tokyo – it takes about six hours to get there by train, bus and boat – so people come there with a very open mind. It's not just something you do on a Sunday afternoon, like having a quick look in a museum. You go with all these people, and it becomes almost a sort of religious experience for the Japanese. Like a pilgrimage to go and experience nature.

How is the Inujima project compared to the other projects on neighbouring islands?

As far as I know Soichiro Fukutake, Japanese billionaire and owner of the Benesse Corporation, started the first of these island projects about 20 years ago. He commissioned the Japanese architect Tadao Ando to build the Chichu Art Museum on the southern island of Naoshima in the Seto Inland Sea of Japan. Then Fukutake had a hotel built, and then another museum, and slowly the whole island was taken over. He invited many artists and architects to build art in the landscape. Then it started to spread, especially during the last five years, to Inujima, and now Teshima, another island. Fukutaka's idea is to try to revive all these industrial islands with seriously declining populations – I think around 20 people live on Inujima, a few more than that on the other islands.

Do the islands feel desolate and abandoned?

Yes and no. It's a strange mix – there were parts that used to be industrial places, like Inujima, or like Teshima, which was a waste dump, and Naoshima, which had a huge refinery. So there's an industrial legacy, which dates from a long time ago but is at this point already been sort of taken over by nature. Fukutaka is trying to bring about this return to nature. On Teshima, for example, he's establishing rice fields again, getting people to come and maintain them, to create a new economy.

Has this new economy been successful?

It has definitely been a success. It's amazing to see these places, where the native population consists only of old ladies, on their little bikes early in the morning, and now there are endless boatloads of young hip Japanese couples who come to visit the art and architecture. It's amazing because year-round, every day of the week, they keep coming. It works very well – it has given a completely new meaning to these islands.

Is it the island's energy-neutral aspect that draws in the people?

Energy neutrality is part of it, but the art is also really important – and the combination of both. For instance, the museum is built to catch the wind, creating a cooling breeze throughout the building. This is experienced by walking through a narrow, cave-like tunnel that opens into a space where all of the works of art slowly move in the breeze. So the energy neutrality is an integral aspect of the work. This is possible because many of these museums promote close relationships between the architect and the artist. Because most of the museums on these islands are made for just one artist or even one work of art, it's possible to create an integrated experience of art, architecture and nature.

—

'BECAUSE MOST OF THE MUSEUMS ON THESE ISLANDS ARE MADE FOR JUST ONE ARTIST OR EVEN ONE WORK OF ART, IT'S POSSIBLE TO CREATE AN INTEGRATED EXPERIENCE OF ART, ARCHITECTURE AND NATURE'

—

EXPLORING
HORIZONS

—

PUSHING THE BOUNDARIES
OF ARCHITECTURE

4

PROJECT
NAI MATCHMAKING

CREATOR
**THE NETHERLANDS
ARCHITECTURE INSTITUTE**

LOCATION
CHINA/INDIA/BRAZIL

TESTIFY!
THE CONSEQUENCES OF ARCHITECTURE

Mumbai's development problems must be addressed from multiple angles

Page
230 / 233

NAI MATCHMAKING
CHINA/INDIA/BRAZIL

THE INTERNATIONAL MATCHMAKING PROGRAMME LITERALLY BRINGS TOGETHER LEADING THINKERS AND DESIGNERS OF THE BUILT ENVIRONMENT TO SHARE KNOWLEDGE AND DEVELOP NEW WAYS IN WHICH TO ADDRESS SOME OF THE WORLD'S MOST COMPLICATED AND PRESSING URBAN PROBLEMS. CROSS-CULTURAL AND CROSS-DISCIPLINARY KNOWLEDGE ARE PUT TO THE TEST IN THE SEARCH FOR COMPREHENSIVE SOLUTIONS.

CONTEXT

People are grappling with urgent spatial challenges in many parts of the world, such as ecological issues, housing shortages, and rising water levels. All of these challenges entail an important task for architecture. The Netherlands Architecture Institute (NAI) aims to identify those issues and to put them on the local and international agenda by means of research and discussion. The NAI does so through the Matchmaking programme, which brings design and challenge together. The NAI uses its worldwide network to connect expertise from every corner of the world and to deploy it to arrive at a solution.

MISSION

The NAI is a museum, archive, library and platform that wants to get people of all ages involved in architecture. The NAI Matchmaking programme currently focuses on three countries: India, Brazil and China. The growth of Asia and South America is cause for a number of complex problems in which architecture can play an important role. The NAI acts in this programme as an intermediary, linking Dutch architects and developers to these issues. The Matchmaking programme takes shape in the form of workshops, debates and realized projects. The project is based on the belief that huge global problems can only be faced by connecting international knowledge, expertise and practice together on a basis of equality.

The programme aims to match Dutch and international expertise with global challenges. Dutch architects are matched up with international architects, mainly in China, India and Brazil, and address issues through developing realizable projects. The Matchmaking project consists of various phases: analysing problems and opportunities in various cities; setting up a local network of architects, theorists and developers; connecting this local network to a Dutch network of international architects; committing a local developer, choosing a site, and developing an actual project; mutually developing this project into a successful case-study. In China phases 1 to 4 have been realized, in India phases 1 to 3 have been realized, and in Brazil phases 1 and 2 have been realized.

REALIZATION

Matchmaking India

With a population of 14 million, Mumbai is the largest city in India. The NAI is focusing on the urban development problems of the city, particularly those connected with slum housing. Work is progressing with a group of Indian architects to design and implement an alternative model for low-cost housing. In September 2009, the NAI invited more than 40 Indian architects and developers to discuss the problem of inadequate social housing, and a group of nine was selected to come to the Netherlands in November 2009 to discuss social housing with Dutch architects and developers and to learn from the Dutch approach. Together with the NAI, they are jointly preparing an international conference on slum housing to be held in Mumbai in December 2010. Various international methods of slum renewal will be discussed during this conference in order to arrive at practical proposals for the situation in Mumbai.

Matchmaking China

The NAI started up its Matchmaking programme in China at the end of 2009, focusing on cosmopolitan cities like Shanghai, Beijing, Shenzhen and Hong Kong, where architects are asked to design and produce buildings at breakneck speed, and there is hardly any time for reflection. By initiating a Matchmaking programme with the key Chinese figures, the NAI hopes to put the major issues of Chinese social housing on the agenda. A group of some ten Chinese architects has been selected, who are matched with Dutch architects in order to jointly formulate a project to be further elaborated in the years ahead.

Matchmaking Brazil

Rio de Janeiro is preparing major infrastructural projects that are being coordinated by decision-makers at an international level, from which the little details and textures of an urban scene cannot be perceived. The NAI 'Unsolicited Architecture' project operates independently and creatively finds clients, sites and a budget to develop alternative solutions to fill the gaps in the system. In the context of a workshop, NAI tried to promote the exchange of ideas between local and foreign architects to identify simple transformations that can improve everyday life. In São Paulo, a joint Architectural Association and Netherlands Architecture Institution (AA NAI) Design Workshop was hosted, to explore the rehabilitation of otherwise obsolete, residual and overlooked urban environments, communities and physical materials, through critical urban analysis seminars, as well as through the use of innovative computational design and digital fabrication processes. With the impetus provided by the 2014 World Cup and the 2016 Olympic Games, the organizers, sponsors and local micro-agencies seek ways in which sports culture can transform troubled urban environments.

Against the backdrop of the discussion surrounding the political dimension of sports today, it is indeed crucial to re-examine the city's infrastructure and the ways in which it can accommodate this influx of people, money and attention. And in order to avoid catastrophic *favela* raids like those preceding the Pope's visit to Rio de Janeiro in 1997 – a step taken to make the city seem safe – serious pre-emptive infrastructural planning measures must be taken.

How did you get involved with the Matchmaking project? I found out about Matchmaking Brazil during a workshop in Amsterdam on slum renewal in Mumbai, India. A delegation of Indian architects was in the Netherlands for the NAI Matchmaking India project. As I had just done my thesis on self-organized urban culture with a case study in Rio de Janeiro, it proved a relevant contribution to the workshop theme during the Matchmaking Brazil iteration.

How did the workshops come together? I was able to participate in all three workshops, which presented three different scales and different specific challenges on site. Every partner involved had their own agendas, which created some necessary tension and kept the debate going. We were discussing the urban agenda in regard to unsolicited architecture, by mapping places and phenomena that are not visible on the city map. We talked about ways to design for these overlooked but vital places, and about everything from how to design water management systems to how to organize micro-revolutions.

Though the whole matchmaking project was organized far in advance, a lot of room was left for on-the-spot improvisation. The participants had to be able to 'go with the flow' and improvise or react to unforeseen developments. It was a very ambitious and intensive (almost killing) eight-day workshop. During the process, the discussion on how to create micro-revolutions, practice socially engaged design, and learn parametric technologies in architecture was central.

NAME
ZINEB SEGHROUCHNI

NATIONALITY
TURKISH

OCCUPATION
URBAN DESIGNER

LOCATION
UTRECHT, THE NETHERLANDS

NAME
RAJEEV THAKKER

NATIONALITY
INDIAN

OCCUPATION
STUDIO X MUMBAI, DIRECTOR

LOCATION
MUMBAI, INDIA

How did the Matchmaking project get started? How did it hope to deal with cross-cultural exchange? Several architects and professionals were invited to a working discussion by the NAI in Mumbai. Ole Bouman discussed the opportunities for sharing and developing a relationship between the NAI and India, in order to formulate novel approaches to research and the engagement of the built environment. The discussion was partially in order to share knowledge previously developed and implemented in the Netherlands, and also to learn from the Indian context to inform new approaches to conventional problems elsewhere. There was mutual trust established from the very beginning of the process, and we tried to address critical issues via our respective environments. The Netherlands is quite far away from India, but what happens in India will affect the Netherlands in five, ten, 20 or even 100 years . . . and vice versa.

What were the goals and what were your personal expectations? I thought we were going to put together a group of experts and practitioners that could help rethink both urban and rural problems. Of course this goal is still being developed, but has not revealed any working solutions at the moment. We have exceeded our expectations in other areas of mutual interest, and this is where the initial meetings have truly sparked the beginning of a conversation that I hope will last, develop and grow towards many collaborations and shared interests.

Overall, did you have a positive experience? It was a positive experience in regards to the openness of discussion. During the exhibition 'Architecture of Consequence' which launched the opening of Studio X Mumbai, Colombia University GSAPP advanced research laboratories interested in studying the future of our cities, which was a tremendous achievement and effort on behalf of the NAI and Studio X Mumbai. The laboratories brought the crises in the economy,

healthcare and natural resources to the forefront of the debate within the conventional global architectural discourse. We hope that this will start a debate within the local context as well ... maybe spawning an architectural response within India itself.

What are your hopes for the future of the project? We have exceeded our expectations in other areas of mutual interest, and this is where the initial meetings have truly sparked the beginning of an enlightening 'conversation' that I hope will last, develop and grow towards many collaborations and shared interests. I believe we need to rejuvenate and open ourselves to ideas and concepts from other parts of the globe. Yes, these places may be extremely different from the context we operate from in India, but accepting knowledge's fundamental ability to transform perception may be our strongest hope for looking towards a positive and beneficial future ... at least in terms of the future of cities.

—

'THE NETHERLANDS IS QUITE FAR AWAY FROM INDIA, BUT WHAT HAPPENS IN INDIA WILL AFFECT THE NETHERLANDS IN FIVE, TEN, 20 OR EVEN 100 YEARS ... AND VICE VERSA'

—

PROJECT
**THE WINTER SCHOOL
MIDDLE EAST**

CREATOR
**MARKUS MIESSEN
AND ZAHRA ALI BABA**

LOCATION
KUWAIT

Students and faculty encounter new viewpoints in a site-specific learning environment

Page
231 / 233 /
238

THE WINTER SCHOOL
MIDDLE EAST
KUWAIT

THE WINTER SCHOOL IS AN EDUCATIONAL PLATFORM BASED IN KUWAIT, USED FOR CRITICAL INVESTIGATION OF ARCHITECTURE AND ITS IMPLICATIONS IN SPECIFIC ITERATIONS IN THE MIDDLE EAST.

CONTEXT

The Winter School Middle East is a localized, small-scale hub that regularly performs cultural and educational activities in collaboration with local NGOs, schools and individuals, and – through its new, long-term presence – houses a critical platform for exchange. Launched as an idea in 2007, the Winter School Middle East was set up as a roaming, mobile institution that has undertaken a series of workshops, seminars, mini-schools and conferences since its inception in January 2008. In 2010, the Winter School moved to Kuwait for longer-term involvement and local engagement regarding creation of a platform for critical exchange.

MISSION

Combining the Winter School's workshop methodology with local initiatives, this intensive workshop-based programme is run with a design- and discourse-led curriculum that combines conceptual and spatial research in the process of radical criticism and the rigorous production of ideas. Students and staff work in teams of up to ten, in which they develop individual and group projects. These projects are tested against the criticism of the group, as well as against the knowledge and expertise of local protagonists. Each tutor-led unit investigates different aspects of the (emerging) spatial realities of the Gulf region, with a strong local and site-specific focus. The curriculum addresses excessive urban development, pollution, unilateral politics and the misuse, abuse and exhaustion of natural resources. It is the hope that artistic and spatial practices will manage and assume responsibility regarding that which politics is often incapable of: outright critique.

REALIZATION

Kuwait is a country in which political parties are banned. Yet throughout recent history, Kuwait's political process has found an indirect form of democratic expression in a deeply-rooted cultural tradition that also corresponds to an architectural typology: the diwaniyah. The diwaniyah is a simple, four-sided room, with seating on each side, in which daily meetings are held; it is a central element of the discursive ritual of Kuwaiti politics, including the consumption of tea and coffee. By providing a platform for facilitating quick communication and consensus building, Kuwait's diwaniyahs constitute an instrument of political expression and debate that in many ways mirrors the role of the newspaper in the West – it is no coincidence that the diwaniyah was of central importance in the struggle against the Iraqi occupation in 1990. Concurrently, the building acts as a form of distributed assembly, where consensus is achieved in small inter-connected groups and societal grievances are broadcast and filtered as they climb the hierarchy of these congregations. It is significant that in the parliamentary elections in 2009, four female candidates won their seats and became Kuwait's first female lawmakers. All four had been visiting those typically male spaces of the diwaniyah prior to the election, a fact that was not always received positively.

The Winter School's interest in the diwaniyah lies in its concrete role as an architectural and spatial typology, which is also a protagonist in the contemporary history of Kuwaiti political life. The diwaniyah is both a real thing and a metaphor. It is an architectural typology whose precise historical role in defining a nation's political identity can be clearly and extensively documented, but it is also the elementary particle of Kuwaiti politics – an unusually crystalline manifestation, in a commonplace and humble architectural form, of architecture's potential as a facilitator of political expression. In the exhibition 'Diwaniyyah: Architectural Space of Political Exchange', at Harvard's Graduate School of Design in 2010, Markus Miessen and Joseph Grima presented a research project exploring the particular situation of the diwaniyah in both theory and material experimentation. Through field-based research and discussion, a spatiopolitical understanding of the diwaniyah was mapped. The diwaniyah was examined as an aesthetic phenomenon and a site of experience. Further, the Winter School project 'Studio Diwaniyah' literally took on the format and physicality of a diwaniyah, focusing on the spatial agency of the structure in the transformation of Kuwaiti life. Within this discursive, social and relational environment, the Winter School students were asked to design, build and implement an enabler and/or disabler of communication. It is the explicit intent that these interventions should stand in an intense reciprocal relationship to each other. Studio Diwaniyah was conceived as a 1:1 experimental laboratory.

Compared to Dubai, the Winter School's first location, Kuwait has been highly urbanized since the 1930s. Its combination of liberalism and open politics presents an interesting starting point, but when it comes to public discursive formats of education, Kuwait only makes use of classical and formalized formats, such as the centralized university. There is an increasing need for the stipulation, development and growth of a local expertise beyond the classic Western notion of urbanism, one that uses the specificities of the local context in order to generate new types of spatial practice. As Kuwait is not at all as consumed and exhausted as Dubai, the serious mistakes made by the emirate can still be avoided.

–
NAME
PATRICIA REED

NATIONALITY
AMERICAN

OCCUPATION
ARTIST/WRITER

LOCATION
BERLIN, GERMANY
–

—
'THEORY CAN BE
TAUGHT TO ONLY A SURFACE
DEGREE I THINK, IN THE END
ONE HAS TO TAKE IT UPON
ONESELF TO REALLY
GET INTO IT'
—

What were your expectations of the project before you arrived?
Since this was the first instance for the Winter School to take place, I went in rather naively and openly, with the idea that on-site some degree of flexibility and adaptability to the situation would be necessary. This was also my first trip to the gulf region, so I went in with the expectation to learn a great deal from our encounters – organized and otherwise. That said, my expectations were basically to give and receive in equal doses, teaching of course, yet learning from the students themselves as well as the various guests that were invited within the scope of the programme.

Exactly what was your experience with the project? I was quite enthusiastic about the interactions we had on-site. We had a mixture of students from the region as well as several European students – all from a variety of backgrounds. The variety of backgrounds makes things slightly more ambiguous when preparing a lecture series that should be relevant to many disciplinary approaches – not using highly specific vernacular or historical precedents to frame the discussion too much in the direction of purely art, theory or architecture. Since the success of the project was wholly contingent on the engagement of the students in relation to the lectures, I sensed a strong degree of reciprocity – and I would qualify my experience positively precisely from this reciprocity of give and take. I was doing theoretically oriented seminars, trying to get students (who were challenged with studio-based projects), to open some perspectives as to the consequences and methodological approaches they might take when examining a particular situation – the seminars were dense and a lot to take in, yet when they come to you at the end of a lecture and ask for references to follow up on, that is generally a good sign. My impressions were that several of the students hadn't yet been confronted with some of the concepts that were outlined, mainly pertaining to politics and aesthetics, but there was a hunger for more, and that sense of curiosity was inspiring.

From the administration side, things were kept rather loose, which at some points seemed like it could have used a bit more structure, but on the other hand it feels more like 'participating' when you know you are welcome to affect the structure of the project – so ultimately this looseness was a gesture of openness to modify and co-create the infrastructure. That said, I never felt that I was merely participating as a predefined cog in the framework, but that I was able to assist in defining what that position would be and how I would move in the system, so to speak.

Do you have regular contact with the other participants? Have you been able to give feedback to them regarding how you thought the process went? Since we are geographically dispersed and the school project had a start and ending date, I don't have regular contact with the other participants in a rigorous way – we keep in touch informally. That said, at the end of session we sat down at a grill-party with the students to discuss with them their impressions alongside our own. Several of the students iterated a request for slightly more structure (never too much!), so that seemed to be a general feeling – that the time for studio development was perhaps, in some cases, too open, with not enough urgency to get things done. From the side of the invited teachers alongside the local organizers, we shall soon again be in touch to reflect and elaborate on our experience through a series of texts and conversations that will be disseminated in some form. The format of the multi-logue/conversation has been an excellent way to cull our reflections and particular biases concerning the study undertaken in the project – I can say for myself, reading the responses and reactions from my colleagues in our conversation has made me see my own blind spots and presuppositions more clearly – so the dialogue itself has been a useful critical tool, even if only selfishly so.

What have the results of the process been? More importantly, for me at least, is hoping that the ideas introduced to the students will penetrate in some way into their production ethos. Theory can be taught to only a surface degree I think, in the end one has to take it upon oneself to really get into it, so my hope is that my result was to have sparked the students with a sense of urgency and inquisitiveness in philosophy/theory, that they will take up on their own – that they experience a wholehearted relevance for incorporating this type of thinking within their practice as designers, artists or architects.

–
NAME
PHILLIP LLOYD ZACH

NATIONALITY
GERMAN

OCCUPATION
ARTIST

LOCATION
FRANKFURT/MAIN, GERMANY
–

How did you learn of the Winter School and why did you decide to take part? In 2010, Markus Miessen held a lecture at the Städelschool where he talked about the Winter School Middle East. It sounded to me like a good reason to get to know a place I did not have any first-hand experience with and simply wouldn't have gone to without a special reason.

I was very suspicious in the beginning – afraid of ending up in a hyper-theoretical and never-ending odyssey of architectural discussions. I hoped for time to do some independent research and also to have a fun time.

What did you find? The overall ratio of the workshop's components was very well-balanced. It started with a few days of highly concentrated introductions, lectures by locals and faculty, guided sightseeing, and talks. That foundation provided a common basis from which a more organic working dynamic followed, framed by a less-concentrated programme.

The common approach was quite product-oriented, in terms of designing a one-to-one solution. That shows how architecture, probably any field of production, is still communicated in today's universities. Having the problematized reality around us led to unforeseen ways of reading space. Talking to locals and walking around the city, we stumbled upon astounding things that led to new ideas. This formed a much deeper understanding of often alienating philosophical texts about politics and space. That experience can only happen in situ, which is what the architects were lacking. Maybe it would be interesting to have a look at Georg Simmel or Rudolf Steiner who, in different ways, also talk about the potential of this kind of interdisciplinary work.

What did you take with you from the experience? The experience opened up new aspects of my personal practice. I am also still in touch with other participants. I hope that it will be possible to develop and keep track of this project. It could be an adaptable model for other educational institutions.

PROJECT
**COPENHAGEN WHEEL /
CO2GO**

CREATOR
SENSEABLE CITY LABORATORY

LOCATION
GLOBAL

Also on page
228 / 233

COPENHAGEN WHEEL / CO2GO
GLOBAL

SENSEABLE CITY LABORATORY'S PROJECTS MESH TECHNOLOGY WITH THE URBAN LANDSCAPE, FINDING NEW WAYS FOR THE AVERAGE CITIZEN TO BE ENERGY- AND SPATIALLY CONSCIOUS. A SMART PHONE APPLICATION THAT MEASURES CARBON USAGE AND A BICYCLE WHEEL THAT GENERATES ITS OWN POWER WHEN NECESSARY ARE JUST TWO OF THE WAYS THAT THE THINK-TANK'S EXPERTISE HAS MANIFESTED ITSELF IN PRACTICAL SOLUTIONS.

CONTEXT

Over the past few years a 'biking renaissance' has begun to transform the urban experience in cities worldwide. Cheap electronics allow cyclists to augment bikes and convert them into more flexible, on-demand systems. This practice, and the Copenhagen Wheel initiative, are a part of a general trend of adding technology to everyday objects to create a 'smart' infrastructure, particularly possible within the dense mesh of the urban environment.

MISSION

Bicycles are very efficient machines. Rather than reinvent them, the idea is to introduce a simple technological enhancement that allows any bike to become a responsive hybrid. The Copenhagen Wheel differs from other electric bikes in that all components are elegantly packaged into one hub. There is no external wiring or bulky battery pack, allowing it to be retrofittable into any bike. Inside the hub are a motor, a 3-speed internal hub gear, batteries, a torque sensor, a GPRS and a sensor kit. Using a technology similar to KERS (Kinetic Energy Recovery System), which has revolutionized Formula One racing, the wheel harvests input energy as it turns. This energy is stored by the battery pack for when the rider needs a boost. The wheel also wirelessly connects to the user's mobile devices. It recognizes its owner upon approach, and allows the rider to lock and unlock

the bike, switch gears, decide when the motor kicks in, and receive real-time alerts automatically. The wheel also has a smart security system: if someone rides away with it, the device goes into a mode where the brake regenerates the maximum amount of power and sends you a text message with its location. As the user rides, the wheel's sensing unit records effort level and information about the surroundings, including road conditions, carbon monoxide, NOx, noise, ambient temperature and relative humidity. This data can be accessed later via phone or web and used to plan healthier bike routes, achieve exercise goals, or meet up with friends on the go.

The sensation caused by the much-awaited Copenhagen Climate Change Conference in 2010, promoted by the United Nations, was more for its failure to reach any consensus than because of the solutions put forth on how the problem of climate change should be tackled.

REALIZATION

The Copenhagen Wheel was unveiled on 15 December, 2009 at the COP15 United Nations Climate Conference. The project was conceived and developed by the SENSEable City Lab for the Kobenhavns Kommune. The prototype bikes were realized with the help of technical partner Ducati Energia and funding from the Ministry for the Environment.

The Copenhagen Wheel is currently in its final prototyping phase and will go commercial in June 2011. The initial prototypes of the Copenhagen Wheel were expensive, but by streamlining the production, the cost of a wheel has been reduced to approximately 600 USD.

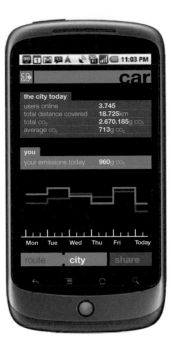

The CO2GO application can track any mode of transportation from your pocket

CO2GO

CONTEXT

According to the Industrial Energy Analysis, transport accounts for a quarter of all global greenhouse gas emissions, and personal mobility represents about two thirds of the total transport energy use. In this context, assessing an individual's personal contribution to the emissions of a city becomes highly valuable. Prior efforts in this direction have resulted in web-based CO_2 emissions calculators, smartphone-based applications, and wearable sensors that detect a user's mode of transport.

MISSION

CO2GO, a new type of smartphone application, is an effective tool that helps individuals make smarter transport choices to collectively reduce carbon emissions in cities. Making sophisticated use of the sensors contained in a standard smartphone, CO2GO deploys an

unprecedented algorithm to calculate real-time carbon emissions while users are on the move.

The backbone of the CO2GO smartphone application is a software engine that collects and interprets data generated by the smartphone's sensors. This combination of data collection contributes to a comprehensive impression of movement and mode of transport. Finally, the data is made relevant to the user by converting it into CO_2 emissions and burnt calories, which it displays on the phone's screen. Travel time, distance covered and associated CO_2 emissions are updated in real-time together with a map view of the user's route.

REALIZATION

Experimental results show that the classification accuracy of the algorithm that CO2GO uses is 82.14 per cent. A working smartphone application for the Android platform has been developed and experimental data have been used to train and validate the proposed method.

–
NAME
CARLO RATTI

NATIONALITIE
ITALIAN

OCCUPATION
**DIRECTOR, SENSEABLE CITY
LABORATORY**

LOCATION
BOSTON, MASSACHUSETTS, USA
–

What is the role of Senseable City Lab in relationship to architecture? At the beginning of the twentieth century, the perimeter of architecture got radically redefined: the new engineering disciplines – dealing with anything from reinforced concrete to steel and glass construction – swept away the old formal paradigms of the Ecoles des Beaux Arts. The whole teaching curriculum had to be redesigned, together with the media that accompanied it. Arguably, we are in a similar condition today, as pervasive computing, ubiquitous handheld electronics, ad-hoc sensor networks, and many new technologies are forcefully entering architectural design and drastically changing the ways in which we understand, design and inhabit space. The perimeter of our discipline is once again being redefined, and this is what we aim to explore.

What distinguishes Senseable City from other think-tank-like organizations? Research by design and design by research: this is how we do projects. We start with a vision of how new technologies are transforming our interaction with the built environment. This is then developed into a partial implementation in the city – what we call an 'urban demo' – which allows us to gather feedback from people and study the impact of the project in creating positive lifestyles. Extensive scientific work follows this phase, where the main questions raised by the vision are addressed. Another interesting aspect is that we work in collaboration with academia, industry and governmental agencies. Also, we do not limit our range of activities to a particular discipline and want to benefit from trans-disciplinarity – from science and mathematics to design and sociology – focused on exploring how bits and atoms, silicon and concrete, digital and physical, can come together in tomorrow's architecture.

—
'MANY NEW TECHNOLOGIES ARE FORCEFULLY ENTERING ARCHITECTURAL DESIGN AND DRASTICALLY CHANGING THE WAYS IN WHICH WE UNDERSTAND, DESIGN AND INHABIT SPACE'
—

What new horizons in architecture can you envision for the future? We envision an 'architecture beyond architecture', at least as we know it today: a new trans-disciplinary field. It will be not just about technology or about tectonics; not just about bits or about atoms, but a seamless blend of the two, in order to support what will remain at its centre. We envision this architecture as performative, intelligent and user-centric – with software seamlessly integrated into hardware . . .

–
NAME
KRISTIAN KLOECKL

NATIONALITY
AUSTRIAN

OCCUPATION
INDUSTRIAL DESIGNER

LOCATION
BOSTON, MASSACHUSETTS, USA
–

How did the concept for CO2GO arise? CO2GO was born of a consideration that underlies many of our projects, which is that today it is very difficult to understand what your impact is in terms of energy or resource consumption. You might close a window or switch off a light, but it's not clear how any of these actions translate concretely to energy reduction. You have a general idea that something you do may consume less or more, but it's hard to know exactly how much. If you are going to make changes in your behaviour, such as your transportation behaviour, you should be able to know what the impact will be.

We wanted to somehow find a way to translate this impact into data that could be looped back to people while they are in the actual process of making decisions – without adding any additional devices. That's how the idea of working with cell phones arose; smart phones in particular already have such a variety of sensors onboard, so we wanted to see if we could mix the data that is already being recorded on a smart phone to automatically identify a user's mode of transport while he or she carries the cell phone in any position.

How does this correlate to a new kind of understanding or feedback with the built environment? You can consider a project such as this as a tool for navigating urban space – a tool that considers all possible modes of transport. It addresses mobility as a mix of any available and adequate transportation choice, combined with the notion that anything we do in cities translates to resource consumption. While cities consume a lot of energy, having compact cities is, on average, a pretty good way of reducing energy consumption. And bringing this awareness to the user can be an incentive for the user to explore his or her transportation choices from a wider perspective, factoring in CO_2 emissions as he would factor in other parameters, like time and comfort level. If people don't have this awareness, they can't make energy-smart decisions. The application should become available to users within one year.

—

'YOU CAN CONSIDER A PROJECT SUCH AS THIS AS A TOOL FOR NAVIGATING URBAN SPACE – A TOOL THAT CONSIDERS ALL POSSIBLE MODES OF TRANSPORT'

—

PROJECT
**METROPOLITAN
PROTOGARDEN**

ARCHITECT
**ECOLOGICSTUDIO /
CLAUDIA PASQUERO
AND MARCO POLETTO**

LOCATION
MILAN, ITALY

Installations engage hands-on interaction with the ProtoGardens project

METROPOLITAN PROTOGARDEN
MILAN, ITALY

**THE INTERACTION BETWEEN TECHNOLOGY, COMMUNITY AND ECOLOGY
IS FOREGROUNDED IN A VIDEO INTERFACE FOR AN IMAGINED URBAN
GARDEN NETWORK AND A SERIES OF RELATED CREATIVE INSTALLATIONS.**

This installation, STEMcloud v2.0, experiments with architectures that produce oxygen

CONTEXT

The 'protoGARDEN' project was commissioned by curator Luca Molinari for an exhibition to be held in Milan's Urban Centre. This exhibition project was initiated by the Minister for Urban and Territorial Development of Milan, to communicate the plans for the future of the city to Milanese citizens, particularly in relation to the expo event that will be held there in 2015. However, unlike typical exhibitions about future projects, this time the municipality commissioned Molinari to put together a group of young architects and engage the public in a new type of dialogue to stimulate new ideas for the future and develop alternative visions of what sustainable urban development might mean.

MISSION

The protoGARDEN project has multiple ambitions. In many ways it aims to be provocative – it refuses to materialize the kind of grand visions that municipalities typically demand, to instead demonstrate the latent potential of existing technologies to allow a re-envisioning of physical space by virtual means. The overall ambition is to reinvent the notions of public and civic service, opening up a forum for novel scenarios that foster ex-

Even though this prototype project is based in the city of Milan, it is meant to serve as an adaptable model interface that other cities can eventually apply as well.

change between citizen-organized initiatives and top-down strategic municipal decisions. Within the proposed scenario, decisions from above can be informed in real-time by the 'urban buzz', via a constant flow of relevant data.

With regard to its users, the project also wanted to be playful and engaging. Various physical installations materialized before, after and during the virtual interface project, which were directly related to the interface but look a more spatial approach in the hopes of directly and physically engaging citizens. It was important from the very beginning to engage the city's 'gardeners' in the construction of their own proto-garden. A good gardener is embedded in the life of his or her garden by allowing an interaction between natural growth and control.

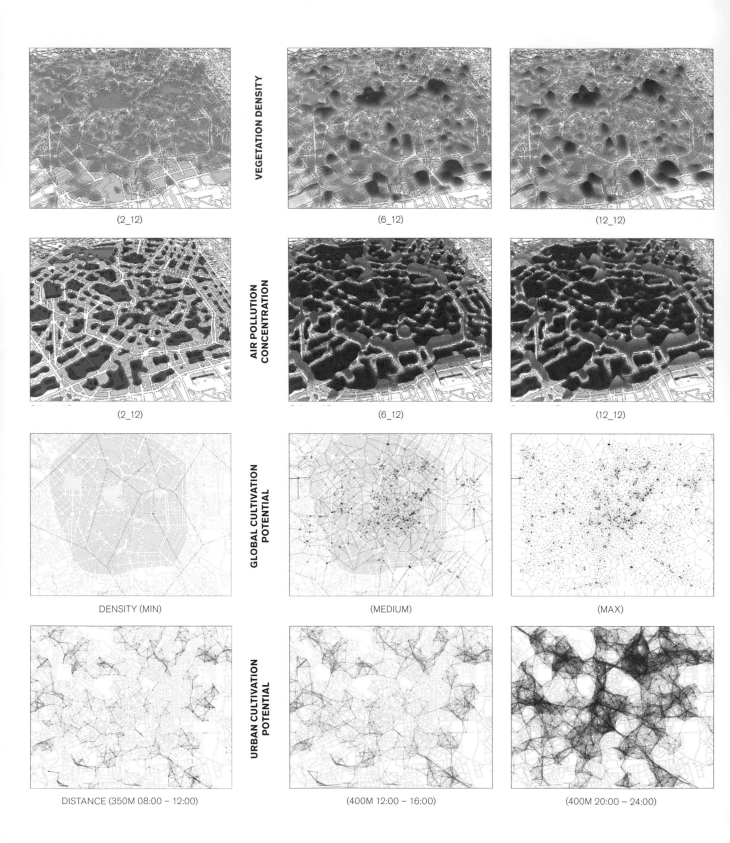

VEGETATION DENSITY

(2_12) (6_12) (12_12)

AIR POLLUTION CONCENTRATION

(2_12) (6_12) (12_12)

GLOBAL CULTIVATION POTENTIAL

DENSITY (MIN) (MEDIUM) (MAX)

URBAN CULTIVATION POTENTIAL

DISTANCE (350M 08:00 – 12:00) (400M 12:00 – 16:00) (400M 20:00 – 24:00)

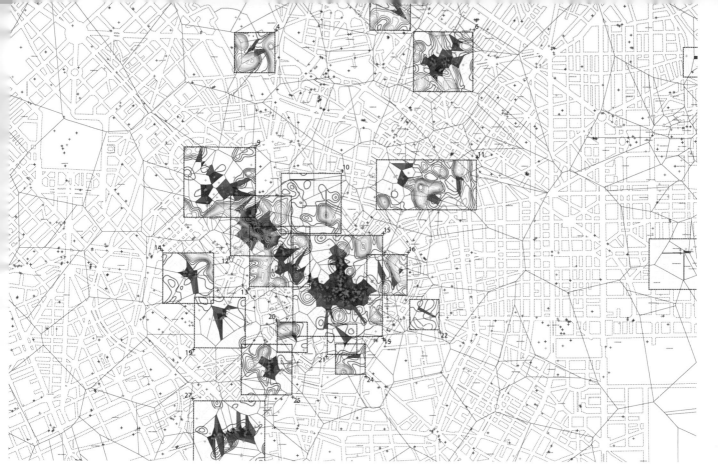

◄ A mapping interface meshes several layers of data relevant to Milan's cityscape

▲ Data mapping allows the city to be segmented in new ways

REALIZATION

The ecoLogic team began by deploying a systemic design framework, operating at the urban scale and mapping multiple operational fields. This process made it possible to visualize the city's dynamic social and ecological systems. The next step was to design a virtual interface with which to represent these urban networks. The interface allows the global and local citizens of Milan to access and 'cultivate' their city as a metropolitan proto-garden made up of virtual plots, fields of urban opportunities and prototypical devices of interaction. The interface, based on a Google maps/Facebook framework, conceivably updates itself in real time, creating a new urban arena capable of constant evolution and adaptation. The hope is that physical prototypes of different natures and sizes will materialize around the city, allowing for diffused and bottom-up actualization of the large-scale plans emerging within the virtual interface. The garden is no longer organic; it is instead a synthetic hybrid, embedded with electronics, remote controls and computational power. The new proto-gardener can nourish the metropolitan environment through his or her daily actions: directly and remotely, materially and digitally, through sensors

This is a prime example of 'neogeography', a diverse set of practices that operate outside, or alongside, or in the manner of, the practices of professional geographers. Rather than making claims based on scientific standards, methodologies of neogeography tend towards the intuitive, expressive, personal, absurd and/or artistic, but may just be idiosyncratic applications of 'real' geographic techniques.

or servomotors. The proto-garden evolves in a performative network that feeds and is fed back by the cultural and social evolution of the metropolis. The presentation of the interface takes the form of a conceptual, explanatory video, as well as various maps, drawings and images that depict and express the potential of the dynamic system.

—

THE NEW PROTO-GARDENER CAN NOURISH THE METROPOLITAN ENVIRONMENT THROUGH HIS OR HER DAILY ACTIONS

—

–
NAME
MASSIMILIANO TARDIO

NATIONALITY
ITALIAN

OCCUPATION
**SCIENTIFIC COMMUNICATOR
OF THE MUSEO TRIDENTINO
DI SCIENZE NATURALI**

LOCATION
TRENTO, ITALY
–

What is your professional background and what is your relationship to architecture and urban planning? I studied Biology at the University of Bologna and did my PhD in Protistology at the University of Pisa. Protistology is a scientific discipline devoted to the study of protists, a group of complex microorganisms. My research thereby generally focuses on the study of lakes (limnology) and in particular on phytoplankton (planktonic algae).

How did your collaboration with ecoLogicStudio arise? How was the initial contact with the architects made? Before the collaboration with ecoLogicStudio my work had no relationships whatsoever to architecture and urban planning. We first met as part of the Alps Biennial of the Alpine and Mountains Landscape in Trento, Italy, which focuses on innovative artistic and research projects in sensitive places and contexts of the alpine European space. The organizers of the biennial basically approached the natural science museum I am working for in Trento and invited us to collaborate with the architects.

Can you describe the process of your collaboration? What was your role, which role did the architects play? We first met in London to discuss the general aim of the project for the biennial. While ecoLogicStudio presented their work and ideas for the installation project, I was able to give some ideas on the envisioned environments that were selected to be presented in the installation, namely ten lakes in the Trentino area, and the possible phytoplankton organisms to grow there. My role was really to take care of the scientific aspects of the project so that it would really work as an experimental incubator. And we did indeed manage to create an incubator that allowed for the insertion and growth of different collected water samples as well as interaction with the visitors.

—
'WE MANAGED TO CREATE AN INCUBATOR THAT ALLOWED FOR THE INSERTION AND GROWTH OF DIFFERENT COLLECTED WATER SAMPLES AS WELL AS INTERACTION WITH THE VISITORS'
—

What do you think did both of you learnt from working together? Did the project have a wider effect on your work as a scientist? What this project had most effect on was my work as a scientific communicator. The core part of my capacity at the museum lies in finding new ways of communicating science to a general interested non-professional public. As part of this outreach, we are trying to mediate the principles of scientific research to non-scientists by producing ongoing research projects and experiments within the museum. The installation by ecoLogicStudio is a great example for an installation that manages to draw a non-scientist audience into a scientific discussion in an artistic way.

–
NAME
MARCO POLETTO

NATIONALITY
ITALIAN

OCCUPATION
ARCHITECT

LOCATION
LONDON, UK
–

How does the ProtoGarden project address architecture? It's an experimental project, but in a way I think it deals with the idea of consequences at its core, by dealing

'IT DEALS WITH THE IDEA OF CONSEQUENCES AT ITS CORE, BY DEALING WITH ARCHITECTURE AS A KIND OF FEEDBACK'

with architecture as a kind of feedback. The main project is the Metropolitan ProtoGarden, which is a video project at this stage. It's a video that acts as a kind of interface. To make the video we went through quite an extensive process of mapping the city, collecting data from the Internet and from various sources and constructing this interface in which users both from Milan and the rest of the world could start to participate in a new interaction with the city. The idea of this kind of interface is the central element of the project, attempting to breach the scale between the individual and the city. Obviously, it takes into account that in that last three or four years, technologies like Google Maps and other similar tools have greatly expanded the possibility of connecting to the city as an organism, as a complex system, while accounting for what the individual sees and experiences.

How do the different parts of the project relate to each other?
Within this kind of interface, we imagined a series of environments, of prototypical spaces within the city, which are the embodiment of this kind of interface. So, on one hand, you can interact from your PC at home, and on the other there are a series of public spaces in the city that would allow a kind of 'cultivation' to happen more physically and directly. These real spaces are what we call the 'prototypes'. In the video they are described

in a way that is a bit diagrammatic, but also by means of images from a series of installations. They can be seen as a self-contained project, but they are part of the same series of experiments that try to materialize what is happening within the interfaces. We can see them as components of this larger idea or project. Some of the installations were made before the video, and some afterwards.

Is this particular interface site-specific to Milan? The video has been constructed in clear relation to Milan, because of the context of this exhibition and the interest that Milan developed after becoming the next Expo site. But it is also a prototypical video – it could be applied to other cities.

What specific Milan-based data do you use? It's a mix. The first set of data has to do more with the environmental conditions of the city. We had data on pollution that was given to us by the municipality, along with traffic and transport data, which we got from a consultant that was based in Milan. There is also data based on the actual vegetation density in Milan, which has been mapped from satellite imagery. The second set has to do with more social mapping, the locations of bars and cafes that we retrieved from Google Maps – in Milan people spend a lot of time in these public social spaces, so this location data is very relevant.

The last set of data comes from Panoramio, another Google plug-in that allows both tourists and citizens to take pictures of the city and geo-tag it.

Then we processed these sets of data through series of algorithms, and formed a group of maps to visualize the emerging networks. Also, for the environmental information, we turned the data into gradient maps that reflect the intensity of these phenomena – for instance the pollution intensity in different parts of the city.

The way you relate to the city can be guided or shaped by looking at these maps. The maps are a conceptual device, but also a functional one. We divided the city into different plots that overlap with the actual city plots, to create a different division of the city, allowing citizens to liberate new areas according to new logics rather than pre-existing ones like private property and boundaries.

Was the mapping a dynamic process, or does it represent one moment in time? The video currently reflects one moment in time. The vision is to eventually make it real-time, and there are groups we are working with, like at MIT, who are trying to develop real-time systems. For now, it acts as a visual and critical framework in which to re-envision the city.

PROJECT
DRIVERS OF CHANGE

CREATOR
ARUP FORESIGHT

LOCATION
GLOBAL

TESTIFY!
THE CONSEQUENCES OF ARCHITECTURE

poverty

drivers of change

ARUP

PRESTEL

▲ The Cards provide a basis for long-term strategizing in Hong Kong   ▼ Arup was selected to present Drivers of Change at Tokyo Designers' Week, 2006

TESTIFY!
THE CONSEQUENCES OF ARCHITECTURE

DRIVERS OF CHANGE
GLOBAL

ARUP FORESIGHT IDENTIFIES THE WAYS OUR WORLD IS MOST LIKELY TO CHANGE IN THE FUTURE – RANGING FROM THE SOCIOCULTURAL TO THE ECONOMIC TO THE POLITICAL TO THE ENVIRONMENTAL. SINCE THEIR FIRST SET OF DRIVERS OF CHANGE CARDS, PRINTED IN 2006, THEY HAVE BEEN PRODUCING AN ONGOING SERIES OF PUBLICATION THAT DEAL WITH KEY ISSUES AFFECTING THE FUTURE OF THE BUILT ENVIRONMENT.

CONTEXT

Arup is a global design and engineering firm and a leading creative force in issues pertaining to the built environment. It was founded shortly after the Second World War by Sir Ove Arup, who introduced the concept of 'total design', in which teams of professionals from diverse disciplines work together on projects of exceptional quality. Arup's Foresight team identifies and monitors the trends and issues likely to have a significant impact upon the built environment and society at large. The group researches and raises awareness about society's major challenges and their implications. Arup also runs events to help clients think more creatively about the long-term future, and to manage risk and uncertainty more effectively.

MISSION

The Drivers of Change programme started as a way for the team to help groups of professionals articulate what they felt was driving change in their fields. Over time, dozens of workshops were held around the world asking the same questions in the same format. The responses were gathered together in a database of information, which is represented in print format as the Drivers of Change cards, a research-based publication developed by Arup to help its business and clients identify and explore leading factors that will affect our world in the future. The publication is a planning tool that helps the user to ask the right questions in order to plan effectively for the future. Certain distinct themes such as energy, urbanization, waste, water, demographics, poverty and climate change recurred globally on a regular basis.

When looking at the context of tomorrow, one has to remember that it will be very different depending on where one is on the planet. It is fundamental for the robust understanding of change that a design method is applied in a synthetic process.

REALIZATION

Each set of cards identifies some of the leading drivers of change that affect our future, trying to help answer the question: 'What will our world be like in 50 years?' Each card depicts a single driver. A factoid and rhetorical question are on one face of the card, backed up by a more detailed exploration of the issue on the reverse. Since the first set of cards was printed in 2006, an ongoing series of publications has been produced that deals with key issues affecting the future of the built environment. The intention is for these cards to act as triggers for discussion, further research and reflection about our future. Each set of cards is arranged and presented within social, technological, economic, environmental and political domains that together are known as the STEEP framework. Drivers of Change serves not only as a vibrant, visual record of research, but also as a tool for developing business strategy, brainstorming and education.

Several test publications were produced for internal use within Arup before being refined and commercially published in 2006. Offshoot projects have included exhibitions at the Venice Architecture Biennale in 2006, Tokyo Designers' Week 2006 and the 2008 Drivers of Change exhibition at Arup's public exhibition space Phase 2 in London. The cards have so far been translated into Turkish, Mandarin and Japanese and have been used in workshops worldwide. Drivers of Change is currently being developed as an integrated part of national strategy in Jordan. Arup Foresight has representatives in London, San Francisco, Sydney and New York.

NAME
MORTEN BENN

NATIONALITY
DANISH

OCCUPATION
**MANAGEMENT CONSULTANT &
PARTNER AT IMPLEMENT
CONSULTING GROUP**

LOCATION
COPENHAGEN, DENMARK
–

How did you find out about the cards, and how do you use them?

I think I've been using these cards since 2006, when they first came out. I'm a managing consultant for a company called Implement Consultant Group. I work with strategy and innovation – those are my two main fields. This client of mine, who works for the Danish Architects Center, knew about Arup, and said these cards are really helpful – helpful in the way they are made, with a fact on one side, identifying the main trend in a given field. I was very inspired by that, so I've been using the cards and boxes for very different things, from environmental strategy to helping a sales academy. They are very useful tools for creating strategic approaches to specific topics, as they provide you with basic facts on these topics. They help when talking about innovative new strategies as well as products, because the cards identify the main things that drive general changes in society – hence Drivers of Change,

I suppose. So if I were, for instance, a producer of pharmaceuticals, or a producer of insulation in the building industry, I'd need to know what is going to hit me, where the change is going to come – what changes will matter the most to me. Against the background of such scenarios, the cards are very useful, in that they allow you to think differently, and to identify important things that you are not accustomed to think about. Normally, a consultant like me would maybe never ask about a demographic challenge or change, for example. But when you're looking at the cards that identify demographic change, you think, yeah, right, this is a real trend that is occurring, and now I will pay attention to it explicitly.

So the cards help highlight underlying factors that people don't always pay attention to?

In the creative phase of any given project, you have a lot of different ideas and opinions going around. One thing we have been focusing on in our company for the last ten years is exactly how to best facilitate meetings like that. We want to make such meetings more constructive and we want to fully involve all the people sitting around the table. When you have people of completely different academic and/or professional backgrounds sitting at the same table, you need something that can spark the collective energy. It is exactly this inspirational impulse that the cards provide. They stimulate everyone to think independently. Creating this kind of interactive brainstorming is much more effective than me standing there with a computer and a projector and presenting a lot of facts to the people. The latter easily bores the hell out of people, and they fall asleep. I'm a firm believer that, most of the time, we already have all the knowledge needed at our disposal, so using these cards basically only facilitates us to come up with the conclusions ourselves and

helps us to evaluate which driver will actually affect our business the most.

Can you imagine a wide variety of other situation in which the cards might be used? Well, I don't think they were intended to be used the way I use them, and at the same time they were exactly intended to be used the way I use them. What I'm saying is that their success lies precisely in their flexibility and adaptability. They're not matched to one given situation, but can be used in any open, innovative discourse that attempts to look into relevant future developments. For the building industry for example, I could imagine them being used in early brainstorming sessions with clients and suppliers, in order to identify which trends and drivers should be considered in the design and building process. Sure, in the end only reality proves which trends and drivers are going to be the dominant players, but we can get pretty close.

–
'NORMALLY,
A CONSULTANT LIKE
ME WOULD MAYBE
NEVER ASK ABOUT
A DEMOGRAPHIC
CHALLENGE OR
CHANGE'
–

NAME
CHRIS LUEBKEMAN

NATIONALITY
USA

OCCUPATION
**DIRECTOR ARUP FORESIGHT
AND INNOVATION**

LOCATION
SAN FRANCISCO, CALIFORNIA, USA
—

Arup's global Foresight, Innovation and Incubation Initiative, explores emerging trends and the impact they might have on the engineering business and that of their clients. How do you picture our future environment and what new approaches are you envisioning? The question is what we are imagining and how we are imagining it. I believe that most of us already have a very good perception inside of ourselves as thinking human beings of any of the challenges that are to come. Our method when we are trying to help others think about the future and understand the future is based on our human needs and desires as they are today, as we anticipate them in the context of tomorrow. But tomorrow is a story, the future is fiction. The story we tell in order to help us understand what might unfold. Very important for us is that it is the gut, the heart and the head, that these three realms at the base create the context of the story that will unfold as tomorrow. We are trying to map all of these factors, a process we call life-mapping or experience-mapping. This world then is the one in which we picture or paint the new experience map. In order to paint the new experience map we have to together create a picture of what the new context, the new world is. So we paint a picture of the context of tomorrow that is always variable using steep categories. They are social, technological, environmental, economic and political.

This is quite a fascinating process because there's never a singularity. One very important thing to me is to remember and to remind others when I am working with them that there will never be one future.

The Drivers of Change box set of cards is a tool for advancing the critical reflection of these various implications. What is the overall structure and intention of this card set? The intention is quite simple. It was to find a way to help participants in our workshops articulate what they felt was driving change for them. It started off as a very simple exercise of literally asking thousands of people again and again the question: What is driving change for you? First we were just listening, then we started to take these answers and catalogue them. Interestingly enough, certain patterns emerged from what people thought would be driving change, no matter whether it was in a city in Africa or in Australia, whether it was in Shanghai, San Francisco or Copenhagen. The topics that kept coming up again and again at the top of the list were energy, waste, climate change, water, demographics and urbanization. We called them the 'big six'. Then in further conversation poverty came up as one of the most fundamental drivers of change. Poverty manifests itself not just at the base of the pyramid in countries such as India or China or the African nations,

—
'BUT TOMORROW IS A STORY, THE FUTURE IS FICTION. THE STORY WE TELL IN ORDER TO HELP US UNDERSTAND WHAT MIGHT UNFOLD'
—

but everywhere. The impoverished are truly everywhere in the world. We took these issues that people felt were driving change and researched and asked further what they really mean and where they intersect. And so these cards became a way in which to pick out 25 issues to force us all to reflect on aspects we might not think of everyday but that are very crucial in certain parts of the world. Later the cards developed a life on their own, we used them in workshops and printed over 20,000 copies of which we gave 10,000 copies to our staff all over the world to make sure that all of our staff were thinking about what was driving change. This way we tried to make sure that they were ready to talk to our clients and to help them to think about change and eventually be then better clients. If we think about the problems we're facing together, then we will demand better solutions in anticipation of the changes – which are coming.

PROJECT
**DECOLONIZING ART/
ARCHITECTURE RESIDENCY
(DAAR)**

ARCHITECT
**SANDI HILAL,
ALESSANDRO PETTI,
EYAL WEIZMAN**

LOCATION
BEIT SAHOUR, PALESTINE

Images from the exhibition 'Oush Grab: Return to Nature'

DECOLONIZING ART/ARCHITECTURE RESIDENCY (DAAR)
BEIT SAHOUR, PALESTINE

DECOLONIZING ARCHITECTURE WAS INITIATED IN 2007, AND HAS BEEN RECENTLY RE-ESTABLISHED AS THE DECOLONIZING ART/ARCHITECTURE RESIDENCY (DAAR). DAAR, BASED IN BEIT SAHOUR, PALESTINE, IS AN OPEN AND COLLABORATIVE STUDIO AND RESIDENCY PROGRAM CREATED TO REPLACE ESTABLISHED MODES OF ART AND ARCHITECTURAL PRODUCTION, MOBILIZING ARCHITECTURE AS A TACTICAL TOOL IN POLITICAL INTERVENTION.

The photomontages suggest a peaceful reintegration of architecture and landscape

CONTEXT

Decolonizing Architecture was initiated in 2007, and has been recently re-established as the Decolonizing Art/Architecture Residency (DAAR). DAAR, based in Beit Sahour, Palestine, is an open and collaborative studio and residency programme created to replace established modes of art and architectural production, mobilizing architecture as a tactical tool in political intervention. The team engages spatial research and theory, taking the conflict in Palestine as its main case study. DAAR's work combines discourse, spatial intervention, education, collective learning, public meetings and legal challenges, in an attempt to open an 'arena of speculation' that incorporates varied cultural and political perspectives. The work of the residency, which takes many forms, is based on a network of local affiliations and an immense historical research archive.

Beit Sahour is a centre of Palestinian political activism. The town played a key role in the First and Second Intifadas, with local activists pioneering nonviolent resistance techniques.

MISSION

The programme is clear and audacious: to reappropriate and transform existing Israeli settlements and military bases, which are among the most powerful instruments of domination. DAAR seeks to avoid two extremes: on the one hand the utter destruction of evacuated structures, as has happened in Gaza, and on the other the reuse of structures for the same purposes as during occupation, which tends to reproduce colonial power relations. Decolonizing Architecture experiments with a third option: 'a strategy of subversion', in which spaces are re-purposed, somehow altered, and invested with new meaning.

DAAR's work does not start from a utopian image but rather from what already exists. It proposes the subversion, reuse, profanation and recycling of the existing infrastructure of a colonial occupation. It employs political, legal and architectural approaches to articulate the contours of a 'detoured' world in which all physical and organizational structures are reused, but not in the way they were originally designed.

TESTIFY!
THE CONSEQUENCES OF ARCHITECTURE

'The Thin Red Line' attempts to visualize the lawless void of the dividing place between three territories

DAAR will not present a unified urban planning proposal Palestine in its entirety, but instead suggests detailed transformations on the architectural scale. There are hundreds of thousands of Israeli-built structures on the West Bank, but because the number of typologies in settlements and military bases are limited – variations on the single-family dwelling in settlements and concrete prefabricated barracks in military bases – these 'fragments of possibility' constitute a semi-generic approach that could be modified to be applied in other evacuated areas.

REALIZATION

At a 2008-2009 show at BOZAR, the Centre for Fine Arts in Brussels, Belgium, Decolonizing Architecture presented itself as an exhibition with the subtitle, 'Scenarios for the Transformation of Israeli Settlements'. Included in the exhibition was a 'manual' determining to what extent evacuated structures in Palestine are flexible to accommodate new uses, and demonstrating the various ways in which they could be adapted or transformed. Two project sites were chosen as two prototypes of decolonization: the colony of P'sagot (still inhabited by colonists) and the former Israeli military base of Oush Grab, which was evacuated in 2006. The production of the manual was based on a series of meetings with the 'stakeholders' in this process: representatives of various organizations, individuals from the local community, members of various NGOs, government and municipal bodies, academic and cultural institutions, local residents, and resident associations. Their genuine participation is crucial, the only engine for implementing the actions outlined in the manual.

DAAR suggests revisiting the term of 'decolonization' in order to maintain a distance from the current political terms of a 'solution' to the Palestinian conflict and its respective borders. The one-, two-, and now three-state solutions seem equally entrapped in a 'top-down' perspective, each with its own self-referential logic. Decolonization implies the dismantling of the existing dominant structure – financial, military and legal – conceived for the benefit of a single national-ethnic group, and engaging a struggle for justice and equality. Decolonization does not necessarily imply the forced transfer of populations. Under the term decolonization, for example, Jewish communities could go and live in the Palestinian areas. Whatever trajectory the conflict over Palestine takes, the possibility of further partial or complete evacuation of Israeli colonies and military bases must be considered.

Zones of Palestine that have been or will be liberated from direct Israeli presence provide a crucial laboratory to study the multiple ways in which we could imagine the reuse, re-inhabitation or recycling of the architecture of Israel's occupation at the moment this architecture is unplugged from the military/political power that charged it.

The project engages a less than ideal world. It does not articulate a utopia of ultimate satisfaction. Its starting point is not a resolution of the conflict and the just fulfilment of all Palestinian claims; also, the project is not, and should not be thought of, in terms of a solution. Rather it is mobilizing architecture as a tactical tool within the unfolding struggle for Palestine. It seeks to employ tactical physical interventions to open a possible horizon for further transformations.

—

THE PROJECT DOES NOT ARTICULATE A UTOPIA OF ULTIMATE SATISFACTION

—

▶ In 1948 the village of Miska (now the West Bank) was destroyed and its villagers displaced; this map represents the region's built-up areas in 2009

TESTIFY!
THE CONSEQUENCES OF ARCHITECTURE

NAME
**ALESSANDRO PETTI,
SANDI HILAL,
EYAL WEIZMAN**

NATIONALITY
ISRAELI / ITALIAN

OCCUPATION
ARCHITECTS

LOCATION
**ISRAEL / PALESTINE /
ITALY / GREAT BRITAIN**
–

What is the organization doing currently? How does it act?

In 2007, after a few years of engaging in spatial research and theory, taking the conflict about Palestine as our main case study, we have decided to shift the mode of our engagement and establish an architecture collective based on a studio/residency programme in Beit Sahour, Bethlehem. Decolonizing Architecture/Art Residency (DAAR) seeks to use spatial practice as a form of political intervention and narration. The projects of the office are based on a network of local affiliations and historical archives we have gathered in our previous researches. Our practice has to continuously engage with a complex set of architectural problems centred on one of the most difficult dilemmas of political practice: how to act both propositionally and critically within an environment in which the political force field, as complex as it may be, is so dramatically distorted in favour of the colonizer. Is intervention at all possible? How could spatial practice within the 'here and now' of the conflict negotiate the existence of institutions, legal and spatial realities without becoming complicit with the unequal reality they produce? How to find an 'autonomy of practice' that is both critical and transformative?

What solutions have you found? What is your most effective approach?

As a response to this problem we suggest revisiting the term of 'decolonization' in order to maintain a distance from the current political terms of a 'solution' to the Palestinian conflict and its respective borders. The one-, two-, and now three-state solutions seem equally entrapped in a 'top-down' perspective, each with its own self-referential logic. Decolonization assumes a process and an action of negation and implies the dismantling of the existing dominant structure – financial, military and legal – conceived for the benefit of a single national-

–

'WE SUGGESTS TO INTERPRET THE TERM DECOLONIZATION AS THE COUNTER APPARATUS THAT RESTORES TO COMMON USE WHAT THE COLONIAL ORDER HAD SEPARATED AND DIVIDED. THE GOAL OF DECOLONIZATION IS TO FIND NEW USES FOR STRUCTURES OF DOMINATION'

–

ethnic group, and engaging a struggle for justice and equality. We propose to interpret decolonization as an act of profanation. To profane, as proposed by Giorgio Agamben 'does not simply mean to abolish or cancel separations, but to learn to make new uses of them'. If sacralisation is the device that separates normal things from its normal use, its opposite movement is to profane. However, to profane is not to secularize. Historical processes of decolonization often reused the buildings and infrastructure left behind in the same way they were designed for, a way that left colonial territorial hierarchies intact. In this sense past processes of decolonization never truly did away with the power of colonial domination.

How is it possible to neutralize the structural power relationship at work then? By reusing structures for new purposes? It is not simply the reuse of the colonial architecture. The dislocation of the power (from an Israeli colony to a Palestinian gated community) is not enough, the aim is to utilize their potential of destruction for new uses, new forms of life. Secularization takes something from the sacred sphere and seems to return it to another sphere, not neutralizing its power. We must neutralize this relation.

How do you deal with the terminology of decolonization? What is the best way to interpret and redefine it? We suggests to interpret the term decolonization as the counter apparatus that restores to common use what the colonial order had separated and divided. The goal of decolonization is to find new uses for structures of domination. The creation of a new use is only possible through deactivating an old use. As such a state of complete 'decolonization' is not the starting point of the projects in the sense of dreaming about the 'day-after' the occupation and other colonial mechanisms have been removed,

but a way of thinking the possible practices of deactivation and reorientation that are folded into the term decolonization, to think them in their 'presentness', within the here and now of the given political/spatial reality. It is a process that never ends. As such 'decolonization' is never achieved, but is an ongoing practice of deactivation and reorientation understood both in its presentness and in their endlessness. A viable approach is to be found not only in the professional language of architecture and planning but rather in inaugurating a collaborative 'arena of speculation' that incorporates varied cultural and political perspectives through the incorporation into the project of a multiplicity of individuals and organizations. An open and collaborative architectural residency programme had thus to replace established modes of architectural production.

What physical projects have you taken on? Through a series of architectural interventions – sometimes pragmatic, sometimes ironic and provocative – we investigate and probe the political, legal and social force fields. By combining discourse, urban intervention, education, collective learning, public meetings and legal challenges, the attempt is to open up the discipline and praxis of 'architecture' – understood as the production of rarefied buildings and urban structures – into shifting network of 'spatial practices' that includes various other forms of intervention.

INDEX

PARQUE EXPLORA
MEDELLÍN, COLOMBIA

Page
56 / 233 / 240

Architect
Alejandro Echeverri Arquitectos

Collaborators
**Architecture:
Isabel Dapena,
Camilo Restrepo Villa,
Sergio Restrepo,
Guillermo Valencia,
Juan Carlos Castañeda,
Maria Andrea Díaz,
Diana Herrera,
Edgar Mazo,
Cesar Rodríguez,
John Aristizabal;
Museography:
Andrés Roldan,
Natalia Pérez,
Felipe Franco,
Esteban Uribe,
Juan Pablo Gaviria,
Sandra Obregón,
Catalina Rojas,
Tomas Arango,
Adriana García,
Sebastián Arias,
Mónica Naranjo,
Antonia Posada,
Isabel Restrepo,
Victoria Estrada,
Franco Oberti,
Camilo Londoño,
Manuel Osorio,
Andrés Goez,
Cesar Arias**

Client
Alcaldía de Medellín

Photography
Alejandro Echeverri

Date
2005–2008

PROJECT ROW HOUSES
HOUSTON, TEXAS, USA

Page
32 / 233

Creator
Rick Lowe (The project has utilized the expertise of many artists, architects, historians, developers, community members, administrators and so forth)

Client
Third Ward community

Developer
Project Row Houses, a non-profit corporation

Collaborators
Many artists, architects, and other community institutions. The main architecture collaborator has been Rice University School of Architecture

Photography
Project Row House

Date
Ongoing

SKATEISTAN
KABUL, AFGHANISTAN

Page
10 / 116 / 233

Creators
**Skateistan /
ACCL, ANOC,
Oliver Percovich**

Photography
**Max Henninger
Noah Abrams (page 10)
www.noahabrams.com**

Date
2007–ongoing

SOS CHILDREN'S VILLAGES LAVEZZORIO COMMUNITY CENTER
CHICAGO, ILLINOIS, USA

Page
144 / 233

Architect
Studio Gang Architects

Engineer
**Structural:
Faz Ehsan of
Thornton Tomasetti
MEP/FP:
Anil Ahuja of CCJM
Engineers, Ltd.**

Client
**SOS Children's Villages
Illinois**

Collaborators
**Jeanne Gang (Lead Design Architect), Mark Schendel (Lead Managing Architect) with Yu-Ting Chen and Beth Kalin (Project Leads) and Lynda Dossey,
Jay Hoffman,
Thorsten Johann,
Boryana Marcheva,
Miriam Neet,
Mauricio Sanchez,
Schuyler Smith,
Beth Zacherle;
Landscape:
Ernest Wong of
Site Design Group, Ltd.**

Photography
Steve Hall © Hedrich Blessing

Elevation drawing
© Studio Gang Architects

Date
2004–2007

THE WINTER SCHOOL MIDDLE EAST
KUWAIT

Page
192 / 233 / 238

Creators
Markus Miessen and Zahra Ali Baba

Photography
Markus Miessen

Date
2007–ongoing

WHERE

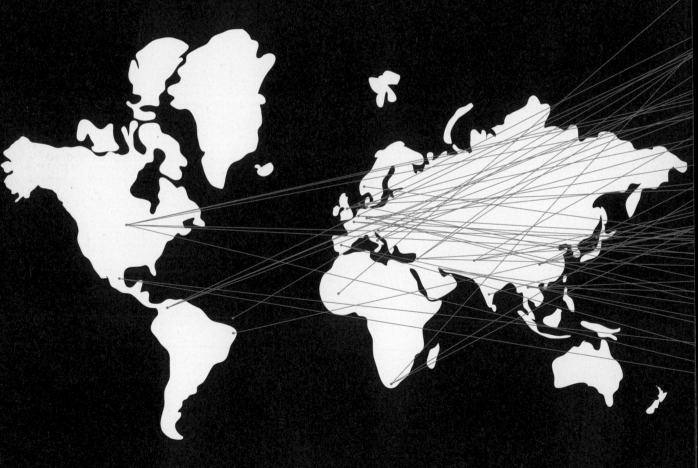

TESTIFY!
THE CONSEQUENCES OF ARCHITECTURE

CREDITS

EDITOR
LUKAS FEIREISS

EDITORIAL BOARD
OLE BOUMAN AND LINDA VLASSENROOD

PROJECT TEXTS
ELVIA PYBURN-WILK

INTERVIEWS
LUKAS FEIREISS AND ELVIA PYBURN-WILK

PROJECT MANAGEMENT
**SUZANNE DE JONG-KOLE
AND SUZANNE PLAUM**

TRANSLATION
PIERRE BOUVIER AND JIAXUAN HUANG

COPY EDITING
D'LAINE CAMP

DESIGN
DE DESIGNPOLITIE

PRINTING
DIE KEURE

PRODUCTION
**MARCEL WITVOET
(NAi PUBLISHERS)**

PUBLISHER
**EELCO VAN WELIE
(NAi PUBLISHERS)**

PAPER
PERIGORD MATT, 115 GR/M²

THIS PUBLICATION
COINCIDES WITH
THE INTERNATIONAL
TRAVELLING EXHIBITION
**TESTIFY!
THE CONSEQUENCES
OF ARCHITECTURE**
BY THE NETHERLANDS
ARCHITECTURE
INSTITUTE

This publication was made possible with the generous support of the Friends of the NAi.

The exhibition was made possible with the kind support of the Dutch Ministry of Education, Culture and Science and the G.Ph. Verhagen Stichting.

MIX
Paper from
responsible sources
FSC® C009115

Although every effort was made to find the copyright
holders for the illustrations used, it has not been
possible to trace them all. Interested parties are
requested to contact NAi Publishers, Mauritsweg 23,
3012 JR Rotterdam, The Netherlands,
info@naipublishers.nl

NAi Publishers is an internationally orientated publisher
specialized in developing, producing and distributing
books on architecture, visual arts and related disciplines.
www.naipublishers.nl

Available in North, South and Central America
through D.A.P./Distributed Art Publishers Inc,
155 Sixth Avenue 2nd Floor, New York,
NY 10013-1507, tel +1 212 627 1999,
fax +1 212 627 9484,
dap@dapinc.com

Available in the United Kingdom and Ireland through
Art Data, 12 Bell Industrial Estate, 50 Cunnington
Street, London W4 5HB, tel +44 208 747 1061,
fax +44 208 742 2319,
orders@artdata.co.uk

Printed and bound
in Belgium

ISBN 978-90-5662-823-9

OLD MARKET LIBRARY, THAILAND
Page 160 / 230 233

TESTIFY!
THE CONSEQUENCES OF ARCHITECTURE

THE WINTER SCHOOL MIDDLE EAST, KUWAIT
Page 192 / 231 / 233

OPEN AIR LIBRARY, GERMANY
Page 24 / 230 / 233

PARQUE EXPLORA, COLOMBIA
Page 56 / 231 / 233

INKWENKWEZI SECONDARY SCHOOL, SOUTH AFRICA
Page 152 / 229 / 233